EAT FOR
Joy

Copyright © 2022 by Susanne Jakubowski

First Edition — 2022

Photographs by Riley Marr Photographs

Cover Design & Interior Design by Indie Publishing Group Inc

Editor: Cassandra Filice

Neither the publisher nor the author is engaged in rendering professional advice or services to the individual reader. The ideas, procedures and suggestions contained in this book are not intended as a substitute for consulting with your physician. All matters regarding your health require medical supervision. Readers should seek personal medical, health, dietary, exercise or assistance or advice from a competent physician and/or qualified health care provider. Neither the author nor the publisher shall be liable or responsible for any loss or damage allegedly arising from any information or suggestion in this book.

All rights reserved.

Anyone interested in reproducing or utilizing any part of this book in whole or in part in any form by any electronic, mechanical or other means or anyone wishing to feature this work may ask permission from the author by contacting the author, at yogawithsusanne@gmail.com.

No part of this publication may be reproduced in any form, or by any means, electronic or mechanical, including photocopying, recording, or any information browsing, storage, or retrieval system, without permission in writing from Susanne Jakubowski.

ISBN 978-1-7781481-0-1 Paperback
ISBN 978-1-7781481-2-5 Hardcover
ISBN 978-1-7781481-1-8 eBook

1. Cooking, Health & Healing, Cancer

I have been blessed with an amazing family and friend network that has supported me through all my crazy ideas and projects. They have kept me motivated and sane through difficult times and help me find joy in the everyday. Thank you to my husband, Michael, and my kids, Roman and Nicholas. Thank you to my extended family, especially my sisters, and to all my "sisters of the heart." Thanks to all my proofreaders who had to endure the beginning stages of the book: Brenda Harper, Carol McNeil, Mary Plata, Brian Smuk, Anne Vivash, Joanne Wilkinson, Pam Howcroft, Laurie Brown, and Tammy Brenn. Thank you to my editor, Cassandra Filice of Write to the End, my publisher, Chrissy Hobbs of Indie Publishing Group, and my photographer, Riley Marr. Special thanks to those who shared their personal journeys with me. I appreciate and applaud your courage.

Contents

Part 1 1

Part 2 27

The Recipes 29

Get Crackin': Eggs 31

    Homemade Mayonnaise 32

    Greens with Eggs 33

    Greek Scrambled Eggs 34

    Best Ever Omelet 36

    Mushroom Quiche 38

    Sheet Pan Sunny-Side Up Eggs 40

    Butternut Squash, Asparagus and Goat Cheese Quiche with Almond Crust 41

Be a Bird Brain: Nuts and Seeds 43

    Crunchy Tahini Chocolate Grain Free Granola 44

    Nesta's Almond Shake 46

    Banana and Blueberry Loaf 48

    Chai Chia Breakfast 50

    Spiced Roasted Pumpkin Seeds 52

    Pumpkin Seed Hummus 53

    Almond Meal Pizza Crust 54

    Walnut, Arugula, and Lemon Pasta 56

    Banana-Coconut Baked Oatmeal 58

    Crunchy Apple Salad with Honey Walnut Dressing 60

    Roasted Curried Chickpeas and Almonds 61

    Wasabi Peanuts 62

    Pecan Nut Butter 63

Green with Envy: Greens and Leafy Veggies 65

    Green Vitamin Packed Juice 66

    Basic Salad Dressing 68

    Tamari Dressing 69

    Layered Jar Salads..70
    Cobb Salad...72
    Creamy Artichoke Dip...74

Crazy about Cruciferous Vegetables 77
    Arugula Salad with Roasted Sweet Potatoes, Caramelized Onions, and Steak ...78
    Low Carb Cabbage Rolls (Vegetarian or Meat).....................80
    Whole Baked Cauliflower with Tahini Sauce and Slivered Almonds ...82
    Honey-Mustard Glazed Brussels Sprouts 84
    Roasted Coleslaw..86

Raving about Root Vegetables 89
    Spiced Carrot Hummus..90
    Roasted Butternut Carrot Ginger Soup 92
    Vegan Sweet Potato Gnocchi......................................94
    Brunch Sweet Potatoes...97
    No Tomato Pasta Sauce...98
    Sweet Potato Shepherd's Pie 100
    Squash and Pumpkin Seed Salad 102
    Carrot Cake with Cream Cheese Frosting 103
    Roasted Carrot and Turmeric Soup 104
    Beet and Ginger Soup...106
    Roasted Beet Salad with Horseradish Cream 108
    Roasted Carrots with Beet Purée, Goat Cheese, and Hazelnuts ...110
    Make Ahead Anytime Dill and Beet Salad.........................113

The Rest of the Rainbow 115
    Asparagus Chopped Salad with Tomatoes 116
    Roasted Tomatoes...118
    Sweet Pea and Asparagus Soup 120
    Asparagus with Lemon-Basil-Yogurt Sauce 122
    Pizza with a Spaghetti Squash Crust 123

Have Fun with Fermented Foods 125
    Overnight Yogurt and Oatmeal...................................126
    Yogurt with Feta Dip...127
    Pan-Seared Tofu..128

I See, You See, We All See Fish and Seafood 131
- Slow-Baked Salmon 132
- Dill, Shrimp and Feta Cheese Salad 134
- Herbed Salmon Burgers with Cucumber-Radish Slaw and Gribiche 135

Make Mighty Organic Meats a Priority 139
- Beef and Broccoli 140
- Turkey Meatballs 144
- Orange Chicken with Brussels Sprouts 146

Beans, Beans, the Magical Fruit 149
- Beans on Toast 151
- Black Bean Dip 152
- Baked Cannellini Bean and Sun-Dried Tomato Dip 153
- Iron-Rich White Bean Dip 154
- Red Lentil and Pepper Dip 155
- Vintage Bean Salad 156
- Lentil Sloppy Joes 158
- Butternut Squash and White Bean Soup 160
- Superfood Soup with Veggies and Lentils 162
- Mushroom Lentil Bolognese 164
- Turkey-Lentil Meatloaf with Orange-Roasted Veggies 166

Beautiful Berries and Fabulous Fruits 171
- Strawberry Rhubarb Compote 172
- Berry Chia Seed Jam 174
- Blueberry Banana Muffins 176
- Orange and Grapefruit Salad 178
- Broiled Grapefruit 180
- Apple Nachos 182
- Diced Avocado Guacamole 184

Devilishly Good Dark Chocolate Desserts 187
- Chocolate Avocado Fudge 188
- Simple Chocolate Ramekin Cakes 190
- Almond Butter Balls 192
- Chocolate Espresso Clusters 194

Tasty Teas **197**
    Lemon Ginger Elderberry Tea 198
    Digestive and Cleansing Tea... 199
    Garlic Tea Tonic 200
    Garlic Ginger Lemon Drink 201
    Blueberry Green Iced Tea 202
    Iced Licorice Tea 204
    Chai Tea Chia Seed Pudding with Warm Apple Topping 206

Conclusion **209**

11 Other Ways to Care for Your Mental Health **210**

EAT FOR *Joy*

Susanne Jakubowski

A Typical Day of Food for Susanne

6:00 a.m. – hot water with lemon and ginger. (I eat the pulp of the lemon, too.)

Breakfast – *The Greek Scrambled Eggs* or *Greens with Eggs* are two of my favourites.

Mid-morning Snack – crudités (carrot, celery, cucumber, snap peas, or any other raw vegetable with hummus or dip.) Try the *Pumpkin Seed Hummus* or the *Iron-Rich White Bean Dip*.

Lunch – A Delicious Salad with Homemade Dressing. Try the *Layered Salad* or the *Cobb Salad*.

Late – Afternoon Snack – Raw Nuts or try the *Roasted Curried Chickpeas* and *Almonds* or the *Wasabi Peanuts*. If supper is going to be late or I need an energy boost, I'll have the Green Vitamin Packed Juice or more water with lemon.

Supper – Soup like the *Roasted Butternut Carrot Ginger Soup* and *Sweet Pea and Asparagus Soup* and a simple green salad. Alternately, I might enjoy *Sweet Potato Shepherd's Pie* or *Slow-Baked Salmon with Roasted Beet Salad*.

Dessert – (Special Occasions) *Apple Nachos or Simple Chocolate Ramekin Cakes*

Introduction: Eat for Joy

Have you ever made the connection between what you eat and how you feel each day?

Your energy level, your moods, your sleep, your libido, and even your success in life are all influenced by your brain's ability to function well. Your brain can't function optimally on junk food and processed foods. A poor diet leads to erratic blood sugar levels, inflammation, and fluctuating hormones, all of which affect how we feel about, cope, and experience life. On the other hand, a healthy diet based on whole foods and natural ingredients helps you to feel joyful and happy.

When we eat well, we feel well!

This book will outline the connection between food and your mental health.

It will explain why you must act now, and give you an outline for how to clean up your diet. I believe that you haven't experienced life fully until you have done so feeling your absolute best each and every day. I want you to wake up every morning feeling energetic and enthused. I want you to enjoy each day free from aches and pains. I want you to be able to ride the rollercoaster of life without depression and anxiety weighing you down. I want you to age backwards, feeling younger and happier every day. I believe this is all possible when you eat well by striving for maximum nutritional value in each bite you take.

My first book, *Fight Fire with Food: Cooking for Cancer Prevention,* focused on eating for physical health. **Eat for Joy focuses on how food affects our mental health**. Change can be hard – even when we *want* to change! Everyone's motivation and determination fluctuates even at the best of times. Committing to a healthy lifestyle is made even harder when our brains are foggy, sleepy, or confused due to malnutrition, toxicity, or sugar overload. In my practice as a holistic nutritionist, I see how many people suffer from issues ranging from mood disorders to anxiety and depression. I also see that as they make different choices at the grocery store, the take-out menu, or the dinner table, their lives change for the better.

My Story

My life changed the day I was diagnosed with triple negative breast cancer, a rare and aggressive type of cancer. The cause of most breast cancers can be attributed to high estrogen, but the cause of mine was mostly unknown. Lifestyle factors and nutrition were indicated as the biggest influences.

Thus, my journey to optimal health began in earnest. I commenced the overwhelming task of researching and studying what is necessary to prevent disease. Thousands of hours of research brought me to the conclusion that food and nutrition affect every cell, membrane, and organ in the body.

You are what you eat is certainly true when it comes to our mental health.

As a child, I grew up eating a pretty traditional diet, in a fairly traditional household where most of our meals were homemade with love and natural ingredients. But processed and convenience foods were just starting to enter the market and the fast-food industry was growing rapidly as the number of working moms continued to increase. Packaged, convenience, and take out foods rapidly invaded our home. Boxed cookies, cereals, chips, and ice cream became staples of our diet. More and more of the ingredients we were using came from a package. For example, macaroni and cheese was made from a box instead of from scratch. Instant pudding, processed cheese spread, and boxed cake mixes now filled our pantry shelves.

Growing up, I craved sweet foods. I ate very few vegetables with the exception of potatoes and carrots. My parents never forced us to eat foods we didn't like. If we didn't want the healthy dinner that was served, we were allowed to make our own peanut butter sandwich on white bread slathered with corn syrup and decorated with raisins. A picky eater, I ate these sandwich suppers pretty regularly. I ate sugar and carbs at every meal. How could I not be addicted?

My body was crying out for help and it eventually rebelled. I spent my teenage years with chronic stomach distress and severe sinus headaches. I didn't cope well with stress, was tired all the time, and was afraid of my own shadow. I was very shy and very emotional. Today, I would likely be diagnosed as having functional depression and anxiety.

Over time, I began to see the role that diet played in my emotional and physical well-being. Leaving home for university meant that I had more control of my diet. I lost 15 pounds in my first year of university and continued to lose weight throughout my time there. I was feeling better as time progressed, but I was still eating a diet of sugar, white flour, unhealthy fats, fast foods, and processed foods. And I topped it all off with a bottle of diet soda every day. I was becoming more and more conscious of the correlation between my physical ailments and my diet. I knew that the heartburn, gastrointestinal distress, headaches, and mood swings were food related – I just didn't know how to stop craving the foods that were killing me. I tried every day to be better and I made strides, but I never came close to feeling really healthy.

The big wake up call came years later. The threat of dying from cancer and not seeing my kids grow up propelled me to action and motivated me to change. My husband and I started researching and fairly quickly realized major changes needed to occur. We started by cleaning out our pantry, fridge, and freezer. Foods containing chemicals, additives, and preservatives were discarded. We focused on eating mostly vegetables, started juicing every day, and gave up all the white stuff. I went from eating only two kinds of vegetables to eating all of them.

The result was huge improvements in both our physical and mental wellbeing. We felt great! Getting through treatment was a challenge for me, but I truly believe if I hadn't adopted this new way of living, I would have been much sicker. Once my treatment was over, my recovery was nothing short of miraculous. My body told me to give up wheat and dairy and this time I listened! The more my diet changed, the more my health improved, including my mental health. It took time but I now have more energy than I ever had, even as a child. I'm emotionally more stable and able to handle stress much better.

Since my cancer experience, I have been totally dedicated to my health plan. It took awhile but I have learned that eating foods that are not healthy for me is not worth the suffering that comes after.

I have learned that when I stick to my plan, I am a happier, more joyful person and I know that you can experience this same benefit from eating well.

"To Begin is the Victory": Success Stories

It's my mission to convince you that food affects our mental health. I would like to share some stories with you of others who have made this connection and changed their lives.

Jill and John's story

A good friend of mine and her husband used to go to parties with friends and always had a good time while there. On the way home, however, the husband would start an argument over something small and it would escalate into a rant about things that were beyond the wife's control. She would be shocked and confused by his words and emotions, so out of character for him. Then they found out through food tolerance testing that he was sensitive to beer and chocolate, which he regularly consumed at these social gatherings. A light bulb turned on. They both felt that consuming these items explained his erratic behaviour. They tested this theory over time, ruining many enjoyable days because one beer or one piece of chocolate cake was consumed. He now stays away from them.

> Alcohol is a huge mood changer. Many people can have one or two glasses but if they cross the line, personality changes occur. They are not necessarily drunk but their brain is affected by the toxins introduced.

In the news….

There's been some press coverage and awareness of how a poor diet can result in people displaying drunken behaviour even though they haven't consumed a single drop of alcohol. Nicholas Hess made the news with his story. When he consumed carbs, he would begin to act drunk. His wife and friends believed that he must be secretly drinking but he swore that no drop of alcohol ever passed his lips. He was eventually diagnosed with "auto-brewery syndrome": a condition where an overgrowth of yeast in the gut turns carbs into gases causing excess alcohol in the blood. Nicholas Hess is not an isolated case and cases of auto-brewery syndrome are becoming more common due to world-wide poor gut health.[1]

Mary's story

When I was a baby and small child, I was never allowed to eat red food dye or concentrated juices, especially orange juice. My parents noticed that when I did, I would have wild temper tantrums. This was my first introduction (although I didn't realize it at the time) to the world of food sensitivities and the dramatic impact they can have on mood and overall health.

At about 11, I went to my first naturopathic doctor who tested me for food sensitivities. I was distraught to learn that my absolute favourite food, white flour, was not good for me. In fact, its presence caused an overgrowth of yeast in my system and was wreaking havoc on my body. At that age (and still, to be honest) my favourite foods were pasta, pizza, sandwiches, chicken tenders – all very white flour-based meals. I was given lists of foods to avoid, consume in moderation, and eat in abundance. As an avid rule follower, this was manageable and within 30 days I noticed a difference in my mood. Those around me noticed as well. My temper and emotions were in a better place, and my sister and I weren't fighting as much because we were both in better control of our emotions.

That diet didn't last for too long though, and over time white flour crept its way back to the forefront of my diet and became my primary reward system. Did well on a test? Pizza! Had a tough day? Mac and cheese – with homemade toasted breadcrumbs on top! During the Covid quarantine, every meal became one of comfort. Like many people, I took up drinking as a quarantine hobby and the combination of comfort foods and alcohol had a huge impact on me. My anxiety and worry became so severe that they were impacting my ability to function. I felt lethargic and yet overstimulated at the same time. It was exhausting. Eventually, I had a full-blown panic attack, which forced me to take a deep look within and re-evaluate my lifestyle choices.

With the help of my "wellness team" I was put on a new food path and supplement regimen. I introduced regular exercise into my life. After eight weeks of following my plan, I saw indescribable improvements to virtually every area of my life. Mental clarity, emotional stability, and even weight loss occurred. Now that I have tasted true, good health, nothing else matters. I'm determined to stick to my plan. I know my mental health depends on it. I now see food as medicine and a source of nourishment. Good food does spark joy.

Dr. Oz

I remember as a teen being stranded in a broken-down car overnight during a trip to visit colleges. All I had for nutrition was a stockpile of potato chips, so I dug in. By the morning, I had no energy and knew my biology had been duped. Now I always carry nuts with me to fend off an energy crash.[2]

Tosca Reno, best selling author and inventor of the *Eat Clean* series

Eating clean, for me, was the ultimate healing tool - a response to my poisoned lifestyle. I had become obese and ill through my own ignorance and overeating habits, consuming vast quantities of processed foods. Unwilling to address my emotions, I did the only "reasonable" thing at the time, eat myself to oblivion. It worked - for a while - until the scale revealed that I was obese and I was flirting dangerously with Type II diabetes and heart disease. I had become ill and depressed. (Vista Magazine Issue no. 125)

Susan's story

I would like to share my experience regarding food and mental health issues. When I was twelve, I experienced a head injury that resulted in a misdiagnosed and mismanaged concussion. I recovered and didn't receive any type of therapy or treatment other than the necessary stitches. To the best of my memory, no scan or X-ray was ever given or offered.

Shortly after this injury, I started to develop panic attacks and unusual stomach and digestive issues. By age 19, I had more intense panic attacks and was placed on a benzo drug to manage them and my anxiety. I was advised to stay on this "low dose" medication permanently as it was a "helpful tool," and to carry on with my life. I tried many times to stop taking it, but it was impossible. It was highly addictive and not an appropriate treatment for a teenaged girl.

After many attempts, I met with a woman who helped me immensely. She connected me to the right people and I was able to successfully wean myself off the medication. It took a very long time to go through this process of withdrawal. I found an organization in England that was working with people to get them off these meds and they had techniques to assist in the management of withdrawal symptoms and the resulting anxiety.[3] They also helped me get to the root cause of the initial anxiety.

Through this organization, I learned the connection between food, blood sugar levels, and panic/anxiety. I learned the impact that protein deficiency can have on your system and how to keep my blood sugar levels steady. I was astounded when I learned of this connection. I changed my diet and felt completely empowered. I made great progress managing my anxiety, depression, and panic and I have used these techniques from the year 1995.

> "In order to change you must be sick and tired of being sick and tired."
> Anonymous

Face the (Food) Facts!

"We live in a paradoxical situation. For centuries, people ate unhealthily out of economic necessity. Now we do so out of choice." (Bryson, 2019). More people suffer from obesity than hunger.[4]

You're not solely to blame for your current state of health. We live in a society of malnourished individuals consuming "Frankenfoods." These are foods laden with chemicals, preservatives, hormones, and pesticides. We're fed misleading information about our health by organizations with ulterior motives and governments and big business who put their profit before our health. Our bodies are rebelling. Sixty percent of individuals in North America have at least one medical condition. Forty percent have two or more chronic diseases, and the rest of the world is not far behind.[5]

As staggering as these statistics are, they don't include the impact on our mental health.

In 2019, the World Health Organization (WHO) reported that mental health, specifically depression, would be the single biggest cause of ill health in the world by 2030.[6] More than 800,000 people die by suicide each year. It is the principle cause of death between those 15 to 19 years old. Our central nervous systems are stressed, causing the stress hormone cortisol to flow through our bodies on a continuous basis. Individuals are in constant fight or flight mode and we're not coping well. One in six people take one or more prescription medications to cope with depression and anxiety.[7] Many others self-medicate with caffeine, alcohol, sugar, and recreational drugs.

The Standard American Diet (SAD) caught up with my family, as it has with millions of others. Of the following list, which is not conclusive, many people experience at least one symptom:

- weight gain
- high cholesterol
- high blood pressure
- diabetes
- gall bladder issues
- ulcers
- headaches
- fatigue
- eczema
- cancer
- mental health issues
- bloating
- gas
- indigestion
- sore joints

The solution is not to reach for some sort of medicine to alleviate the symptom. That doesn't get to the root of the problem, which is often points to what we're eating. The more we mask the symptoms without exploring the cause, the more likely new symptoms and illnesses will appear.

Food is the first medicine we should address.

Even as late as the 1960s, it was not understood that the brain plays a role in what we choose to eat. It was always believed that the stomach dictated our food choices. The invention of the gastric bypass showed doctors and scientists that the stomach was only part of the equation. Removing the stomach does not kill off the appetite or stop cravings. Operating on the stomach does not change what is going on in the patient's brain.

Nutritional psychiatry is the study of your brain on food. It's based on the simple premise that what you eat affects the structure and function of your brain, and therefore, your mood.

Researcher Roy Wise from McGill University set out to prove that the brain was *not* what drove us to eat, and he ended up showing the opposite. He wired rats' brains to be stimulated in the area that corresponds to emotions and decision making. When the rats were given a slight charge, they took great interest in food and would eat until the stimulation was stopped. Then they would drop the food and lose all interest. Not only did this show the huge role the brain plays in what we eat and how much, he also discovered that hunger, or the desire to eat, can be turned on and off with a snap of the fingers.[8]

In 1944, the legendary expert on human nutrition, Ansol Keys, conducted the *Minnesota Starvation Study*. This involved feeding thirty-six healthy males two meager meals a day and only one meal on Sunday for a six-month period. The men were given 1500 calories a day. During the experiment, the subjects' average weight dropped from 152 to 115 pounds. More important, the men became irritable, lethargic, depressed, and were more susceptible to illness. This was believed to be due to the depletion of nutrients. The subjects were malnourished. As they returned to a normal calorie count, they recovered their vitality, proving that the amount of food we consume and the nutrient content it contains are important to our mental health.[9]

Scientists have studied how dietary patterns impact mental health and how specific nutrients affect us on a biochemical level and alter our brain chemistry. They have also studied how the gut and brain are linked.

Dr. Daniel Amen, the only psychiatrist and brain disorder specialist to actually take scans of the brain to determine treatment, has stated that the brain shrinks with both poor diet and obesity. The larger and heavier you get, the smaller your brain becomes. He's observed how the actual tissues of the brain change with poor nutrition. Inflammation and malnutrition have been shown to affect mood and cause depressive symptoms while also playing a major role in severe mental illness.[10]

This connection between mood and food wasn't and still isn't recognized by many doctors and specialists even though several studies have made this connection. In fact, seventy-eight percent of doctors don't feel comfortable talking about nutrition.[11] Eleven million people a year die from eating bad food and not enough fruit and vegetables.[12]

What we are now recognizing is that food matters.

Harvard Health Publishing reviewed studies comparing the traditional American diet to the Mediterranean and traditional Japanese diets. They found that the risk of depression on the American diet was 25 to 35 percent higher than those who ate the Mediterranean and Japanese diets. The consumption of more vegetables, fruits, healthy protein, and unprocessed grains were cited as the reason.[13]

A study out of the United Kingdom published in the *Central European Journal of Public Health* studied food consumption and stress and concluded that the frequency of eating unhealthy foods was positively associated with perceived stress in females and depression in both males and females.[14]

The effects of probiotics on mental health are being widely studied. A recent study evaluated the difference between pregnant women given a probiotic, *L. rhamnosus*, between 14 and 16 weeks of gestation and those who weren't, and found that those taking the probiotic had a significantly lower incidence of postpartum depression and anxiety.[15]

In recent news, a Quebec professor has developed a ketogenic drink containing MCT oil. It was marketed as a product to treat cognitive impairment that leads to Alzheimer's and dementia. He had been researching the effect of ketones on the brain for quite a long time.[16] Dr. Mary Newport has written several books on her experience using coconut oil to treat her husband with dementia with remarkable results. She went on to do formal studies with other candidates who had the same or similar results.[17] Both studies concluded that MCT oil can reverse and prevent dementia.

Did you know that a typical human has approximately 100 billion brain cells, with an average of 1000 synaptic connections per cell?

Food and Energy Levels

Did you know that the most common reason women go to the doctor is because of a lack of energy?[18] A survey conducted for *Dr. Oz Magazine* found that seventy-four percent of respondents said they find themselves wishing for more energy almost every day. Fifty-nine per cent would rather have more energy than drop a dress size and 79 per cent would rather have more energy than have more sex. Low energy levels are a direct consequence of poor eating habits. Fifty-three per cent of the respondents in the study said they tend to eat more when low on energy and thirty per cent reach for sweets to give them energy. (doctorozmagazine.com). Added preservatives and chemicals in food, such as inorganic phosphate, anticaking agents, and artificial colouring and flavourings, exacerbate the situation. While these chemicals are approved in small quantities, the effect of eating packaged food is cumulative. The more you eat, the less energy you'll have.

Food and Hormones

Hormonal imbalances can sap energy, happiness, and mental focus. They can also cause more severe symptoms of irritability, depression, anxiety, mood swings, acne, bloating, breast tenderness, food cravings, headaches, poor sleep, and acne. Contributing to this condition is a high-sugar diet consisting of refined carbohydrates, caffeine, stress, dairy, factory farmed meat, and dairy containing hormones and xenoestrogens. The latter are synthetic chemicals found in the environment that mimic estrogen in the body. Plastics, pesticides, chemicals, and many pharmaceuticals are xenoestrogens that are close enough in molecular structure to estrogen that they can bind to estrogen receptor sites with potentially hazardous outcomes.

There are many ways that what we eat affects our hormones:

- A high-sugar diet full of chemicals puts stress on your liver. The liver is the body's detoxification powerhouse. When it's not functioning properly due to a fatty liver, toxicity, or xenoestrogen overload, hormonal imbalance occurs.
- Eating poorly leads to the disintegration of the gut lining, which leads to a disruption in the absorption of amino acids, which are the building blocks needed to produce hormones.
- The thyroid regulates your metabolism, controls the way your body uses energy, and keeps your hormones in check. If you're lacking in magnesium and iodine the thyroid can't fulfill its role.

- Healthy oils ensure that the stress hormones, cortisol and adrenaline, don't go into over production, and medium-chain triglycerides help with the elimination of excess estrogen and progesterone balancing the body's hormones.
- Testosterone deficiency is a precursor to irritability. Foods to eat are parsley, leafy greens, salted almonds, coconut oil, bone broth, apple cider vinegar, fermented foods, and wild salmon.

Food and Personality

Ayurveda, the ancient study of medicine from India, states that food has the power to change your identity. Practitioners believe that food becomes blood and the blood flows to the brain. The brain is sensitive to these changes in chemistry and directly results in changes to your personality. Therefore, you truly are what you eat. Each food has mood changing chemicals. As these chemicals accumulate in our brain our personality changes can become chronic or repetitive. For example, Ayurveda practitioners believe that hot chili creates anger and passion, cheese incites depression and confusion, and kale promotes a feeling of emotionlessness and disconnection. They recommend that you choose foods that balance your constitution. A simple test helps you determine your constitution and the diet you should be following.

Food and Anxiety and Depression

We know that we need vitamins and minerals not only to survive, but also to thrive. These vitamins and minerals cause chemical reactions in the body that create other chemicals like the "feel good" hormones that affect our brain and influence our mood. Studies show that certain enzymes in food boost our serotonin levels. Eating nutritiously influences our levels of motivation or our "get up and go" and our ability to take care of ourselves. Potassium chloride in normal amounts is said to be safe but that's assuming you're eating it in small quantities – if you eat numerous packaged items a day, you're not eating a small quantity. When this occurs, it has the potential to slow down cardiac activity leading to lethargy and a drop in motivation.

Food and ADHD, Autism, and Mood Disorders

Although the jury seems to be still out on whether disorders like ADHD and autism are caused by dietary deficiencies during pregnancy, some connections have been made. Folic acid and iron have been studied and a connection made between these disorders and the microbiome. One thing we do know is that food has a huge influence on the symptomologies of these disorders and their severity. Sugar, caffeine, artificial additives, and allergens all influence behaviour and intensify symptoms of these conditions.

Food and Alzheimer's and Dementia

Numerous studies have linked dementia to what we eat, our inability to metabolize sugar, and any nutritional deficits. Dementia and Alzheimer's are now referred to as diabetes of the brain. Lack of B12, D, magnesium, and niacin are just some of the vitamins that have all been found lacking in those with impaired cognition. Food is an important factor in determining how fast your brain ages. Overeating and weight gain are also factors causing dementia.

"We shouldn't be looking exclusively at the brain to explain mental illness nor should we be looking at the digestive system solely to explain irritable bowel disease. You can't possibly have a large brain unless you've got the energy to fuel it." (Lieberman, 2019, as cited in Bryson, 2019.)[19]

A No-Brainer: The Brain-Gut Connection

Nothing in the body works in isolation. Your body is influenced by the health of your gut and its microbiome, defined as your personal makeup of good and bad bacteria. Our body is made up of bacteria: little bugs or organisms that can live in diverse environments like our guts but that are also plentiful in our mouth, nose, ears, intestines, genitalia, and skin. There are more than 10,000 species of microbes and each contains its DNA. Most live in our digestive area and support every aspect of our health and wellbeing. These intestinal organisms determine the functioning of our immune system, detoxify, reduce inflammation, and are neurotransmitters and vitamin producers. They impact nutrient absorption, tell us when we're hungry and full, and help us utilize carbohydrates and fats. These organisms determine what ailments we take on, from allergies to cancer, and affect our mood, our perception of the world, and even the clarity of our thoughts.

What kind of bacteria do you have? The good type that helps us digest our food properly and get the right nutrients, or the bad type that causes infection and disease? We need the good bacteria to outnumber the bad bacteria, but in the majority of people today the diversity and abundance of bacteria is lacking. This "gut rot" affects our central nervous system (the system that determines if we feel stressed or calm) and our ability to absorb or create all the previous mentioned chemicals, vitamins, and minerals.

A healthy gut is vital for mental health and overall well-being. In fact, the gut microbiome may be the most important organ in your body.

The good news is you can change the bacteria in your gut using simple dietary modifications as outlined in this book and steer the course of illness and disease.

As you read further, you'll see that brain-healthy foods are also gut-healing foods. They contain fiber or prebiotics that feed the garden in your gut, and probiotics that contain good bacteria. There are foods with nutrients that assist us in digesting our foods and healthy fats that reduce inflammation and heal leaky gut. Each food in the recipes is chosen with the intent of healing your gut, and therefore, your brain. The happier your gut is the happier you will be.

Note: if you want to assess the health of your microbiome, some background information will make it easier: how many antibiotics have you been on throughout your life; did your mother take antibiotics when she was pregnant; were you born by C-section; breastfed; have ear or throat infections growing up; have you used steroid medications like inhalers; do you use acid-blocking remedies/drugs; or have food allergies? All these factors influence your gut health.

Have I convinced you that our brains and our ability to enjoy life is affected by what we consume?

If I have, then the next step is to recognize what our brains need to function optimally. Our goal is to provide it with the proper nutrients preventing malnutrition, and keeping inflammation levels low.

The Chemicals that Keep Us Balanced

We have a system in our bodies called the central nervous system. It has two branches: the sympathetic system controls our fight and flight system and the parasympathetic system controls our relax and renew system. Unfortunately, these days most of us are in a low-level state of agitated sympathetic functioning. The feeling of being "on" all the time leads to feelings of anxiety and agitation that further stress our nervous system. In response, the body sends in natural steroids and adrenaline to combat the stress. Your immune system, perceiving threat, will send out cytokines (messengers) that put your body on high alert. The result of these messengers is inflammation. Your diet, if poor, is a stressor and exacerbates this process. Therefore, we can see that food creates an immune response and it is this constant attack on our nervous system that leads to disease.

All disease is first caused by inflammation and your immune system controls the amount of inflammation in your body.

Our body also responds to stressors by releasing cortisol, the stress hormone, into our system. Continued cortisol release wears us down and leads to adrenal fatigue or shut down. Now we are stressed *and* exhausted. Food matters.

Our brain and central nervous system work together and they need to be in balance.

Serotonin is a neurotransmitter. It sends signals between our nerve cells and the rest of the nervous system. It regulates our mood, our appetite, and our ability to get a good night's sleep and it influences our cognitive abilities like thinking and reasoning. Low levels of serotonin are associated with anxiety and depression. There are actually more receptors for serotonin in the gut than in the brain. This is why scientists are now calling your gut the "second brain." It's producing serotonin. Experts are now realizing that changes in diet are more effective than common antidepressant drugs.

Dopamine is another important brain chemical/hormone that influences happiness. It's referred to as the "feel-good" neurotransmitter that sends information between neurons. Dopamine is released when we do enjoyable things like eat or have sex, resulting in feelings of pleasure and satisfaction. Poor diet and health can lead to dopamine deficiency, resulting in diseases such as depression and Parkinson's, and too much can lead to mania, hallucinations, and schizophrenia. Too much dopamine can also play a role in addictive behaviour and anxiety disorders.

Oxytocin is a chemical messenger secreted by the pituitary gland. This gland is found at the base of the brain and is often referred to as the "love hormone." It contributes to our emotional well being and our ability to bond with others, especially our babies. Lack of this hormone can lead to feeling emotionally low and lacking the desire to socialize. When we're stressed and cortisol levels rise, oxytocin drops. Diet plays an enormous role in production of this hormone. We need foods containing vitamins D and C, magnesium, and healthy fats to keep our oxytocin levels balanced. Eat mushrooms, peppers, tomatoes, spinach, and avocados.

Norepinephrine is also called noradrenaline. It functions in the brain as a neurotransmitter and hormone. Along with adrenaline it increases heart rate and blood pumping from the heart. It provides us with the "fight or flight" response in a dangerous or stressful situation, and lowers blood pressure, helps to break down fat, and increases blood sugar in an effort to send more energy to the body. It also helps fight depression and is instrumental in keeping us motivated. Certain foods increase this neurotransmitter in the brain: beans and legumes, bananas, oatmeal, fish, and meats. Also effective are exercise, cold showers, and a good night's sleep.

GABA is the chief inhibitory neurotransmitter in the central nervous system. In other words, it reduces excitability, which is why it's used to treat anxiety, ADHD, and mood disorders. Zinc and B6 are required for synthesis and regulation of GABA. You can increase your GABA intake by adding fermented foods to your diet. Foods rich in probiotics synthesize GABA in the gut. *Lactobacillus rhamnosus* is a specific strain that's been shown to be effective.

The Major Nutrients

The brain uses nutrients at 10 times the rate of any other tissue or organ in the body. Nothing works in your body without nutrients. When there are deficiencies, the brain is the first to display symptoms such as insomnia, anxiety, and depression. It's commonly a combination of imbalances, deficiencies, and overloads that cause mental illness.

Vitamin D is one of the most important supplements. Vitamin D is a hormone that's been called a "neurosteroid" because of its impact on the brain. It's also an anti-inflammatory, which is a key factor in its efficacy; a large component of mental issues can be attributed to inflammation. Vitamin D plays a role in the production and maintenance of the feel-good hormones dopamine, oxytocin, and serotonin. It also affects the hypothalamic-pituitary-adrenal (HPA) axis, the system that's responsible for how we adapt to stress.

Clinical trials have supported supplementation as an effective treatment for depression and anxiety. A 2016 study on young women with PMS moodiness significantly decreased anxiety, sadness, and crying with D supplementation.[20] Another study looked at those with more severe depression. They gave a high dosage – 50,000 units – per week for eight weeks to severely depressed individuals and saw improved symptoms compared to the placebo.[21] Further studies have examined the role of vitamin D along with pharmaceutical drugs like fluoxetine. Researchers found significant improvement with vitamin D-fluoxetine combination by the fourth week of treatment.[22] Postpartum depression has also been shown to be linked to low levels of vitamin D.[23] Foods containing vitamin D are fatty fish such as mackerel and salmon, beef liver, cheese, egg yolks, and white mushrooms. In order to get the optimal levels of this vitamin, supplementation of 5,000 to 10,000 IU daily may be required, especially if you live north of the equator.

Magnesium is an important mineral. First, vitamin D can't be absorbed without it. Second, it's a factor in over 300 enzymatic processes in the body and is particularly important in dealing with stress because it encourages serotonin production. It's often called the "anti-stress" mineral because it helps relax muscles and aids in sleep. It can be found in leafy greens, nuts, seeds, and unrefined whole grains.

Fish oil: Omega 3s Fish-derived omegas contain eicosapentaenoic acids (EPA) and docosahexaenoic (DHA), which have a well-documented anti-inflammatory effect on the brain. EPA lowers cortisol and has shown to be as effective as the drug fluoxetine for lowering depression. (Daniel K. Hall-Flavin, M.D, Mayo Clinic Newsletter, https://www.Mayoclinic.Org/diseases-conditions/depression/expert-answers/natural:remedies-for-depression/faq-20058026). It seems to be effective for mood, bi-polar disorder, and depressive symptoms but not major depression. Like vitamin D, it seems to work well with anti-depression drugs like citalopram or fluoxetine.

Omega 3s are found in fatty fish such as salmon, sardines, mackerel, herring, cod, and lake trout. Non-fish sources are walnuts, flaxseeds, mixed greens, soybeans, and tofu. Supplementation of 4,000 mg is recommended for the average person.

Omega 6s and 9s are essential fatty acids that play a role in brain development. Although the omega 6s can be found in healthy foods like nuts and seeds, meat, poultry and eggs, they're also found in very toxic vegetable oils – particularly corn oil – that are used in processed and restaurant foods.

Omega 9s are found in organic olive oil and help reduce cardiovascular diseases and cancer. They may also improve insulin sensitivity and decrease inflammation. The body can produce this nonessential fatty acid on its own so supplementation is rarely necessary.

B vitamins are one of the most important vitamin groups for brain health. Out of the 13 essential vitamins that our body needs to function properly, eight are B vitamins. These eight are chemically distinct nutrients that play an important role in our overall health, our brain, and our nervous system. Our cells need them for energy and our brain needs them to manufacture neurotransmitters. B1 (thiamine) helps release carbs from our food and keeps our nervous system healthy. B6 (pyridoxine) is involved in brain processes and development as well as immune function. Deficiency in any of the B vitamins can cause anxiety and irritability. The best sources are organ meats and whole grains.

B6 or pyridoxine is an essential cofactor in the development of the central nervous system. It helps the body make the hormones serotonin and norepinephrine. It's also involved in making hemoglobin, the protein in blood that carries oxygen to the body and the brain. It helps your body make melatonin, which regulates your internal clock and your sleep. Studies suggest that deficiencies in B6, along with B12 and folate, play a role in memory and cognitive decline and cause depression in seniors.

B3, niacin or niacinamide Vitamin B3 helps break down nutrients into energy. It affects all our body's cells and influences metabolism. It's a powerful antioxidant that makes sex and stress hormones and boosts brain function. A minor deficiency can result in depression, apathy, and anxiety, and a severe deficiency can lead to dementia and even death. You can get B3 from beets, fish, liver, peanuts, eggs, milk, and dairy.

B12 or cobalamin A water soluble vitamin that is involved in the metabolism of every cell in the human body, B12 plays a huge role in our mental health. Deficiency causes a host of psychiatric symptoms including anxiety, panic, depression, and even hallucinations. B12 deficiencies trigger a nervous system and red blood cell response.

Vitamin C has a therapeutic and preventative effect on mental illness. It protects the neurons against oxidative stress, alleviates inflammation, regulates neurotransmission, affects neuronal development, and controls epigenetic function. All fruits and vegetables contain vitamin C but those with the highest content are cantaloupe, oranges and citrus fruits, kiwi fruits, berries, broccoli, red pepper, sweet potatoes, winter squash, and tomato.

Probiotics are found in fermented foods. They replace and restore gut bacteria. As mentioned earlier, a healthier microbiome results in a healthier brain due to increased absorption of vitamin and mineral intake. Probiotics reduce inflammation and permeability of the gut and directly regulate the production of serotonin in the brain. Consume cultured dairy products (yogurt), fermented soy (miso, tempeh), coconut products (kefir), or fermented foods (sauerkraut).

Prebiotics are compounds found in food that stimulate the growth of probiotics. They work together to enhance the gut microbiome. Examples are onions, asparagus, bananas, and pomegranates.

Iodine is a mineral that's essential for brain development. A lack of iodine can cause significant irreversible mental impairment. It's a necessity for healthy thyroid function. Deficiency leads to hypothyroidism with symptoms such as fatigue, depression, anxiety and brain fog. It can be found in fish (cod and tuna), seafood, seaweed, eggs, dried prunes, dairy, and added to table salt.

Iron needs to be at the right levels for the brain to function properly. Too much can cause oxidative damage and cell death and too little can cause damage to brain structures even after levels are restored to normal. Those with iron deficiency may display a variety of mental health issues including anxiety, irritability, depression, and poor concentration.

Zinc is a mineral that activates hormonal, neurotransmitter, and signaling pathways in the gut that control brain functions including cognitive functions, depression, anxiety, emotional stability, our social ability and our mood. Appetite and sleep are also influenced by zinc levels. Too little zinc can cause panic attacks. It can be found in beef, oysters, seafood, lamb, and organic eggs. Supplementation is often needed to reach optimal levels.

L-Theanine is an amino acid found in green and black tea leaves. It increases alpha waves in the brain that promote relaxation and assists falling asleep. It's often prescribed for people with psychological disorders, including bipolar. The drug version is known as Gabapentin, which has significant side effects. L-Theanine is an excellent anti-anxiety agent, inducing calmness while maintaining the ability to focus. If you wake in the middle of the night, you can take more without a fear of overdosing.

Tryptophan is another essential amino acid. It balances nitrogen in the body. It creates niacin, which creates serotonin and eventually converts to melatonin. It's often taken as a supplement (5-HTP) for insomnia, sleep disorders, anxiety, ADHD, and teeth grinding. It's found in foods that are high in protein such as eggs, chicken, turkey, tofu and soy, yogurt, chocolate, pumpkin and sesame seeds, and fish.

Foods to Avoid

The nicknamed SAD (Standard American Diet) diet is the norm for most of North America and is taking over the world. These Frankenfoods are destroying our brains. Food scientists work on the perfect combination of fat, sugar, and salt to make their products irresistible to our palates. The finished products produce the same effect on our brains as cocaine. In fact, it has been said that sugar is even *more* addictive than cocaine. Our society lives for their next hit.

Below is my list of foods to avoid.

Foods with caffeine reduce blood flow to the brain. Common culprits are coffee, certain teas, and chocolate. Using caffeine to get through the day, especially when we're exhausted, just causes more exhaustion and increased cortisol levels.

Alcohol lowers blood flow to the cerebellum – the part of the brain associated with physical movements and coordination. It makes the brain smaller, increases the risk for Alzheimer's and other dementias, contributes to memory problems, and worsens depression and anxiety.

Sugar is the leading cause of inflammation, and therefore, of almost all disease in the body.

Processed food is any food that's been altered from its natural state. It usually involves adding high levels of sugar, fat, or salt to increase its appeal and almost always includes artificial flavourings, vegetable oils, preservatives, and chemicals. If you don't recognize the food as coming from nature or don't recognize the ingredients, it's probably a chemical addition.

White flour is refined and nutrient deficient. It causes congestion and slows down digestion and metabolism. The result of consumption is often weight gain, stress, headaches, migraines, and constipation. It is a leading cause of bowel diseases and autoimmune disease.

White rice is basically sugar and has the same effect on the body as eating pure table sugar. It lacks protein and contains arsenic, which is carcinogenic, so moderation is key, especially for children. If eating rice pasta, try pasta made from brown rice, lentils, and quinoa.

Processed corn and soy are highly refined and contain high levels of pesticides. Most commercially grown corn is GMO (genetically modified) and contains dangerous glyphosates. Both are hard to digest even in their organic, natural state. The corn and soy that are used in almost every processed food on the grocery shelf are so highly refined that the body doesn't recognize them as real foods.

Vegetable oils are toxic and devoid of nutrients. Corn, soy, canola, safflower, and sunflower are highly refined. The oils are usually extracted through chemical solvents and are toxic. The plants they come from are usually full of pesticides and glyphosate and are genetically modified (GMO).

Conventional meat products and processed meats have been fed grains such as GMO corn and soy (carbohydrates) that help fatten the animals. Pesticides, herbicides, fungicides, and fertilizers are often used in their feed and end up stored in the animal's fat where we, in turn, digest it.

Animals in factory farms are often treated poorly and slaughtered inhumanly. It has been said that when killed in this manner, they release hormones and chemicals that are found in the meat. Most processed meats such as bacon, lunch meat, and jerky contain nitrates. Studies have shown that they may contribute to mania or hyperactivity and promote symptoms of schizophrenia. Buy organic whenever possible.

Pesticides and toxins in food should be avoided as much as possible. One way to do this is to avoid whenever possible buying non-organic produce. The **"Dirty Dozen"** is an annual list that names the fruits and vegetables found to have the most pesticide residue. The most recent list includes strawberries, spinach, kale, collard greens and mustard greens, nectarines, apples, grapes, cherries, peaches, pears, bell and hot peppers, tomatoes, and celery. The least toxic are revealed in a list called the **"Clean 15"** and include avocados, sweet corn, pineapples, onions, papayas, frozen sweet peas, eggplants, asparagus, broccoli, cabbage, kiwis, cauliflower, mushrooms, honeydew melons, and cantaloupes.

Should I Avoid Gluten?

Gluten is a protein found in wheat, barley, rye, and often oats. It is one of the leading causes of the "leaky gut" referenced earlier. The wheat we eat today is overabundant in powerful inflammatory proteins called gliadin, which causes the imbalance in gut flora. The lining of the gut should be strong and tight, keeping food, waste, and microbes inside the intestinal tract; however, gluten causes destruction of the gut resulting in gaps where food and toxins can leak into the blood stream causing inflammation. People who are celiac must avoid all gluten because the body attacks the small intestine leading to severe reactions. Others have a gluten sensitivity that causes headaches, bloating, and gas. Wheat is sprayed with glyphosate and then calcium propionate is added in the manufacturing process of making breads, and both these additives cause behaviour and brain issues.

I recommend eliminating gluten from your diet to avoid the inflammation and disease that go along with it.

Gluten free grains, flours, and starches that are better for your brain

amaranth	arrowroot	bean flours	buckwheat	cassava
chestnut	chickpea	millet	nut flours	certified organic oats
quinoa	sorghum	taro	teff	yucca

Not-so-good for you flours

corn	white rice	potato	tapioca	soy

Flours containing gluten

all purpose white wheat flour	barley	bleached flours	bulger
cake, pastry and bread	couscous	durum	farina
graham	kamut	malt	matzo
tabbouleh	wheat berry	wheat bran	spelt
whole grain wheat flour	semolina	faro	

Read the label… These foods may contain gluten (and they definitely contain additives!)

artificial extracts	Asian sauces	bacon	baking powder	barbecue sauces
marinades	bouillon cubes	brown rice syrup	caramel colour	
graham	kamut	malt	matzo	
dextrin	flavourings	gravies	plant or vegetable protein	
licorice	imitation crab	miso	MSG	
mustards	processed meats	prepared broths, soups, and stews		
sausages	seasonings	vegetable gums		

Are Lectins the Next Gluten?

There has been a lot of trash talk lately about lectins. It's been said that they're toxic and cause inflammation. Lectins are carbohydrate-binding proteins found in such plant-based foods as potatoes, beans/legumes, grains, rice, tomatoes, eggs, dairy, and peanuts. The theory is that because these plants produce a toxic chemical to protect themselves in nature from predators – insects, fungi, molds, and diseases – we ingest those toxins when we eat them. The truth is that our bodies need a small number of lectins for cell interaction, but consumption of large amounts can cause digestive distress. Research suggests the elimination of lectins can help diminish symptoms in those with autoimmune diseases such as rheumatoid arthritis, diabetes, and celiac disease.

When some lectin-containing foods are cooked the lectins become inactivated or weakened. So, if you like foods with lectins, cook, soak, sprout, or ferment them. Make sure you soak your beans, soy and kidney beans especially, overnight and boil in fresh water before consuming. Rice and oats can be purchased in their sprouted form. Although you can't completely eliminate the lectins in your food, you can lessen them and make these foods easier to digest and safer to eat.

Foods to Eat

The foods that I recommend are prebiotic, probiotic, fermented, low carb, gluten free, and contain healthy fats. They are mood boosting foods that contain magnesium, flavonoids and phytonutrients, vitamin D, and the nutrients that are listed above. I have divided these foods into those you should eat every day and those you should eat in moderation.

Eat these everyday and in unlimited quantities:

Leafy greens All leafy greens and lettuces including dandelion greens, boston or butter head, iceberg, loose leaf, romaine, endive, radicchio, frisee, escarole, Mache, mesclun, and purslane. People who eat fresh greens one to two times a day have cognitive abilities comparable to those 11 years their junior.[24]

Cruciferous vegetables This grouping includes broccoli, cabbage, cauliflower, arugula, watercress, Brussels sprouts, bok choy, radish, turnip, kohlrabi, rutabaga, maca, horseradish, and daikon. These vegetables are full of phytochemicals, fiber, vitamins and minerals.

Non-starchy vegetables This group of vegetables is particularly high in vitamins and minerals and are of the non-starchy, lower sugar variety: onions, mushrooms, artichoke, green beans, celery, asparagus, garlic, leek, fennel, shallots, scallions, ginger, parsley, and water chestnuts.

Low sugar fruit In this group we include avocado, bell pepper, cucumber, tomatoes, zucchini, squash, pumpkin, lemons, and limes.

Berries are higher in sugar content than other fruits, but they are the are also higher in vitamin C, fiber, and antioxidants. Blueberries in particular are superstars, full of phytonutrients called flavonoids, which fight depression and protect the brain from free radicals. This category includes raspberries, blackberries, strawberries, elderberries, bilberries, acai, cranberries, Goji, and currants.

Fermented foods This category includes yogurt, kefir, sauerkraut, kimchi, fermented vegetables, meats, fish, and eggs. Yogurts should be full fat, organic, and unsweetened.

Fats Healthy oils should be unrefined, cold-pressed, virgin or extra virgin oils from avocados, coconuts, olives, and flaxseeds as well as grass-fed organic butter and ghee. I cannot stress enough the need to stay away from unrefined oils such as corn, canola, soy, safflower, and sunflower oils.

Nuts and seeds Nuts, in general, are healthy fats that are full of antioxidants, vitamins and minerals, and vitamin E, which fights off Alzheimer's disease. Many nuts and seeds are high in magnesium, potassium, selenium, and essential amino acids. Eat raw nuts, not roasted, salted, or sugar-coated varieties.

Legumes (beans, peas, peanuts, lentils) Legumes are full of fibre and antioxidants and are a good source of protein. Legumes keep your blood sugar stable and enable you to burn more energy.

Whole Eggs are one of the most nutritionally complete foods you can consume. The yolk and white compliment each other and are meant to be eaten together. They have high levels of B6, B12, choline, iron, and folate, which are all good for the brain. They're also a great source of protein.

Herbs and seasonings There are no restrictions in this category, but especially important are turmeric, ginger, sage, parsley, and rosemary. Read the ingredient lists as many seasoning packages have gluten, fillers, or preservatives in them.

Herbal teas and tisanes Teas can leave you feeling both alert and calm. They are full of bioactive compounds called flavonoids, which have a positive effect on cardiovascular health. The polyphenols in tea counteract age-related decline of brain function. Green tea has been studied for its ability to disrupt the buildup of plaque in the brain. Holy basil or Tulsi tea, turmeric and ginger teas, chamomile, and rooibos teas also have brain healthy properties.

Bone broth Bone broth is a source of collagen, glycine, and glutamine – all compounds that heal our gut lining. It is rich in minerals to keep our bones strong. You can drink a cup of stock a day or use it in soups, sauces, and gravies. Add some apple cider vinegar to your stock pot to draw the collagen out of the bones.

Foods to Eat in Moderation

These are foods that can be eaten in small amounts everyday or a couple of times a week.

Root vegetables Found in this grouping are sweet potatoes, beets, carrots, taro, turnips, and cassava. Beets have been promoted as one of the healthiest foods that you can eat for their ability to reduce inflammation. They're high in antioxidants and nitrates, which increase blood flow throughout your body and brain.

Whole grains Whole grains are full of fiber, B vitamins, folate, iron, and magnesium. They're an essential source of time-released energy. It's important to choose your grains carefully. Only eat whole, unrefined grains such as oats and brown rice. Ancient and sprouted grains are better for us. Try amaranth, buckwheat, millet, spelt, kamut, and quinoa in moderation.

Grass-fed organic meats and wild game Full of protein and omega 3 fatty acids, organic meats are better for us than factory farm meat. Organic meats are a good source of omega 3 fatty acids, antioxidants, essential amino acids, and have less cholesterol than regular meats.

Dark chocolate Good quality, pure chocolate (at least 85%) without sugars and fillers is full of protein, fiber, antioxidants, and flavonoids. Chocolate reduces cortisol levels and is anti-inflammatory. It does contain caffeine, so limit your intake if you're sensitive.

Apple cider vinegar Buy this vinegar in its organic form with the "mother": strands of protein, enzymes, and friendly bacteria that sit on the bottom of the bottle. It's antimicrobial and known for its high levels of antioxidants. It's a strong prebiotic and has digestive benefits.

Whole fruits Oranges, grapefruits, apples, kiwi fruit, pomegranates, pineapple, avocados, mangos, watermelons, olives, and bananas are all full of fiber, antioxidants, and are loaded with minerals and vitamins. They should be eaten in moderation as they're a source of natural sugar. Too much sugar, no matter the source, isn't good for our brain or body.

Occasional Foods

These foods are packed with nutrients but have a down side so should be consumed once a week or a couple of times a month.

Wild fish and seafood Fatty fish such as mackerel, salmon, sardines, and trout all have healthy omega 3s, but before heading to the fish market there are some caveats to consider. Plastics in our oceans, mercury in our lakes, and antibiotics and dyes given to farmed fish all pollute this excellent source of nutrition. Only buy wild fish preferably from line caught operations. Most tuna is just too toxic to consume due to pollution in our oceans. Seafood has also been found to contain micro plastic particles that are now being found in humans. Check your local fishery guide for information regarding your locally caught fish.

Kale, spinach, and Swiss chard These leafy greens are full of nutrients but they also contain oxalate, which can cause kidney stones. Steve Grundy, author of *The Plant Paradox*, believes that kale is poisonous to the body because it's hard for us to digest. I like to eat these greens in moderation and also in the baby or young varieties.[25]

Peppers, eggplant, tomatoes, and white potatoes This grouping is part of the nightshade family. They are full of powerful nutrients but many people believe that they contain substances that may cause irritable bowel and other autoimmune conditions. Inflammation seems to be the symptom associated with consuming too much.

A little bit about water and its importance

Although it's not a food per se, I'd be remiss if I didn't mention the importance of water to the health of our brain. Even mild dehydration can hamper our mental health, impacting mood, energy, and focus. A common first symptom is a headache, but irritability, impaired cognitive function, and even delirium can follow. Studies have shown that when you're dehydrated even a simple task seems overwhelming and motivation to do that task declines the more dehydrated you are. Conversely, if you drink eight glasses of water a day you can increase your focus and reaction time by 30 percent (Moscani, 2019, p. 260).

Cooking Your Own Food Can Be Fun and Healthy

"Cooking is a lost survival skill"[26] (Cowther, 2015).

If you learn some of the basics of cooking, you can create your own meals quite easily.

When you cook for yourself, you control what goes into your body. It's the best way to improve your diet. A John Hopkins study revealed that people who make their own meals twice a week take in fewer calories, unhealthy fats, and sugars than those who cook once a week or less.[27] When you cook at home you can control portion size and the quality of ingredients. Restaurants generally use the cheapest products they can find because profit margins are low.

Cooking is easy, fun, and saves you money, but most important, by learning to cook you will be actively participating in your own health and wellbeing.

To take some of the challenge away from cooking your own meals from scratch, follow some basic guidelines:

- A little preparation makes cooking easier and faster. Invest in some good knives (chef, serrated, and a paring knife) and a wood cutting board. Proper measuring spoons and cups are important as well.
- Before you start cooking, clear your space and have your ingredients handy. The French call it *mise en place*. If you are using a recipe, read the whole recipe from beginning to end. Note the time it takes and the tools needed before starting. I can't tell you the times I've started a recipe just to find out I was missing main ingredients, or it takes a day to marinate, or only serves four and I have eight coming for dinner.
- Choose to cook with fresh, ripe, whole, and local foods whenever possible. Hard to find ingredients often discourage us from trying a recipe. Keep it simple and you won't be disappointed.
- Get your friends and family involved. Make it a social time and reinvent the family meal instead of letting it be a hurried affair where everyone eats at a different time. Turn off the television and put away the phones.
- Try some basic meals first that you don't need a fancy recipe for such as salads, sandwiches, burgers, pizzas, stir fries, and soups and stews.

The Recipes

The recipes in this book, like my previous book, *Fight Fire with Food: A Cooking for Cancer Prevention,* are made with ingredients that are easy to find, easy and quick to make, and contain nutrients and ingredients that will make you feel joyful after consumption. Most of my clients can't believe how easy it is to eat well and how their lives change when they switch to clean, low inflammatory foods that keep their gut and their brain healthy.

Get Crackin': Eggs

One egg has 70 calories, six grams of protein, two grams of saturated fat, and 185 milligrams of cholesterol. Eggs are full of nutrients such as lecithin, a type of fat found in cell membranes, and choline, an essential nutrient that aids brain development. They contain compounds that have anti-inflammatory and antioxidant properties. I recommend you buy organic, free-range eggs. Local farms are a good source.

Homemade Mayonnaise

This mayonnaise recipe is used in several of the recipes throughout this section. It only takes a few minutes to whip it up and it's healthier and lighter than store bought versions. Key advantage: It doesn't contain any chemicals or preservatives.

Makes 1 cup (250 ml)

- 1 cup (250 ml) extra-light olive oil
- 1 large egg
- 1 large egg yolk
- 1 tablespoon (15 ml) fresh lemon juice or red wine vinegar
- 1 teaspoon (5 ml) Dijon mustard
- ⅛ teaspoon (2.5 ml) sea salt
- Pinch of ground white pepper

Place all ingredients in a blender and blend until emulsified. Add garlic, spices, horseradish, or hot sauce for flavour.

Greens with Eggs

If you've never had cooked spinach or kale, let me tell you it's a real treat! Heating the greens brings out their rich flavour and makes them easier to digest. Two cups of greens seem like A LOT... but there's a lot of shrinkage that takes place. Try adding a little chopped garlic to the oil.

Serves 1

- 2 teaspoons (10 ml) olive oil
- 1 cup (250 ml) baby spinach
- 1 cup (250 ml) baby kale
- 2 tablespoons (30 ml) grated Pecorino cheese (sheep)
- 1 large egg
- Salt and pepper
- Hot sauce (optional)

Heat 1 ½ teaspoon (7.5 ml) oil in a non-stick skillet over medium heat. Cook spinach and kale, stirring, until just wilted, 1 to 2 minutes. Transfer greens to a plate, and sprinkle with 1 tablespoon (15 ml) cheese. Heat remaining ½ teaspoon (2.5 ml) oil in a skillet over medium heat. Crack in egg, and cook until white is set.

Serve egg over greens. Top with remaining cheese and drizzle on hot sauce if using. Season with pepper.

Greek Scrambled Eggs

This scrambled egg medley is a great alternative to a vegetable omelet, which is a staple in my house. I love Greek salad and spices. With this recipe I get to enjoy these flavours for breakfast.

Serves 6

- 6 organic eggs
- 2 ripe plum tomatoes, diced
- ¼ cup (60 ml) Kalamata olives, diced
- ¼ cup (60 ml) water
- ½ cup (125 ml) goat or sheep Feta cheese
- 1 tablespoon (15 ml) extra-virgin olive oil
- 2 cloves garlic, finely chopped
- 2 cups (500 ml) baby spinach
- Sea salt and black pepper to taste

In a medium bowl, whisk together the eggs and then add in the tomatoes, olives, water, and feta.

In a large pan, heat the olive oil over medium heat. Add the garlic and cook for one minute or until lightly brown. Add the spinach and cook for one more minute.

Add the egg mixture to the pan and toss with a spatula for 2 to 3 minutes. Eggs should be fluffy and tender, not runny. Add salt and pepper to taste.

Best Ever Omelet

Omelets are a great way to get in your protein and vegetables for the day. They're quick and easy to make and helpful in using up leftovers. Feel free to substitute the vegetables here for any you prefer. It used to feel strange to eat vegetables for breakfast but now it feels strange not to (and of course, omelets can be eaten for any meal!).

Makes 1 large serving

- 1 tablespoon (15 ml) unsalted butter
- 1 ounce (28 g) onions, chopped
- 1 ounce (28 g) mushrooms, chopped
- 1 ounce (28 g) red bell pepper, chopped
- 2 to 3 eggs, medium size
- 2 tablespoons (30 ml) milk or milk substitute such as coconut milk
- Salt and pepper to taste
- ½ ounce (14 g) shredded cheese (goat or sheep)

Melt half the butter in a medium skillet over medium heat. Add vegetables and sauté until soft, 5 to 7 minutes. Remove from the pan and set aside.

In the same pan, melt the remaining butter. In a small bowl, whisk together eggs, milk, salt and pepper. Coat the entire bottom of the pan with the butter by tilting and swirling the pan. Add the egg mixture and move it in the pan until it covers the pan evenly.

Cook without stirring. As the eggs begin to set, use a spatula to gently push the eggs away from the sides of the pan so the egg mixture in the center can get to the edge.

When the entire egg mixture is set, add the vegetables on top of one half of the omelet. Sprinkle half of the cheese over the vegetables. Gently fold the omelet in half to cover the vegetables and top with remaining cheese.

Mushroom Quiche

I'm a lover of everything mushroom for both taste and health. I could eat them for every meal! Mushrooms are rich and full of fiber, protein, and antioxidants, and are super low in calories. This quiche doesn't have the traditional pastry as the crust. Instead, the zucchini and onion are the base. This is great for a brunch and any leftovers can be had the next day for lunch. Serve with a fresh green salad.

Serves 4

- Avocado oil, for greasing the baking dish
- 1 cup (250 ml) zucchini, shredded
- ¼ cup (60 ml) onion, diced
- ¼ cup (60 ml) blanched almond flour
- 6 large pasture-raised eggs
- 1 cup (250 ml) sliced mushrooms
- ½ teaspoon (2.5 ml) garlic powder
- ½ teaspoon (2.5 ml) freshly ground pepper
- ¼ cup (60 ml) unsweetened non-dairy milk

Preheat the oven to 350°F (177°C) and grease a 9-inch (22.86 cm) round baking dish with avocado oil.

Extract the excess moisture from the zucchini by wrapping it in a large paper towel or clean kitchen towel and squeezing, discarding the liquid. Combine the zucchini with the onion and the almond flour in a medium bowl. Add the zucchini-onion mixture to the prepared baking dish and press it down to form a flat crust.

Bake the crust until it begins to cook and crisp a bit, about 8 minutes. (Don't skip this step or the crust will be soggy.)

In a medium bowl, whisk the eggs. Stir in the mushrooms, garlic powder, pepper, and non-dairy milk.

Pour the filling over the crust and bake until the eggs are fully cooked and not jiggly, 15 to 18 minutes.

Serve warm. Store any leftovers in an airtight container in the fridge for up to 5 days.

Sheet Pan Sunny-Side Up Eggs

This is a brilliant idea for when you have to cook for a crowd. It's easy, no-fuss cooking and you can serve everyone at once.

Makes 12 eggs

- 12 large eggs
- 1 tablespoon (15 ml) avocado oil, butter or ghee
- Sea salt and pepper

Preheat the oven to 425°F (218°C).

Place a half sheet pan in the oven and preheat for 10 minutes.

In a bowl, carefully crack all the eggs into a large measuring cup or bowl with a spout.

Remove the sheet pan from the oven and drizzle with oil or butter, spreading the fat over the total surface. A pastry brush works well. Carefully pour the eggs into the pan.

Bake until eggs are desired doneness, 5 to 6 minutes for runny yolks, 8 minutes for firm yolks. Sprinkle with the desired amount of salt and pepper.

Cut each portion and serve by lifting with thin spatula.

Did you know that the traditional white chef's hat has as many pleats in it as ways you can cook an egg?

Butternut Squash, Asparagus and Goat Cheese Quiche with Almond Crust

This quiche is good for any everyday meal and fancy enough to serve to guests. It has some of my favourite healthy ingredients like asparagus, squash and almonds. The first time I made this quiche I used too small of a pie plate and found the crust too thick. Make sure you use a full size quiche dish. It is grain free and gluten free but the crust can also be left out entirely, changing the recipe to a crustless quiche.

Crust

- 2 cups (500 ml) almond flour
- 1 large egg, beaten
- 2 tablespoons (30 ml) minced fresh sage
- 2 cloves garlic, minced or crushed
- ¼ teaspoon (1 ml) each salt and ground black pepper
- 2 teaspoons (10 ml) organic unsalted butter

Filling

- 1 cup (250 ml) peeled and diced butternut squash, roasted
- 4 or 5 spears asparagus, cooked until just tender
- 5 large eggs
- ⅓ cup (80 ml) (full fat milk or milk substitute)
- ¼ teaspoon (1 ml) sea salt
- ½ to ¾ cup (125 to 175 ml) soft goat cheese
- 8 fresh sage leaves, optional

Preheat the oven to 400° F (205 C). Prepare the crust. Grease a quiche pan with olive oil cooking spray or melted butter. In a large bowl, whisk almond flour, egg, minced sage, garlic, salt and pepper. Melt butter and mix into the mixture. Press dough into the bottom and up sides of the quiche plate. Bake until the crust is lightly golden, 10 to 15 minutes.

Prepare filling by whisking eggs, milk and salt.

Place squash in the prepared crust, top with egg mixture and drop goat cheese into eggs. Top with asparagus and sage leaves if using.

Bake until the centre is set, 15 to 20 minutes. If the crust edges are browning too much, cover with foil.

Be a Bird Brain: Nuts and Seeds

Nuts are nature's superfood and a great snack to carry with you to satisfy hunger or feed a craving. They're full of beneficial fats and high in protein. Studies show that nut eaters are healthier and live longer than those who abstain. Nuts lower inflammation because of their high levels of polyunsaturated fats, fiber, vitamin E, and phenolic properties.

Almonds are high protein, high fiber nuts that help control weight gain. They're heart healthy and help lower blood sugar levels. They're also good for the gut because they help strengthen good bacteria.

Brazil nuts are amazingly good for your mental health. Eating just one Brazil nut provides you with 100 percent of your daily needs of selenium, a nutrient needed for a healthy immune system and for thyroid health. They're also anti-inflammatory.

Macadamia nuts are high in calories but also healthy monounsaturated fat – even higher than avocados. These types of fats may lower your risk of heart disease and improve the function of your blood vessels. They lower your insulin levels and help with blood sugar control.

Walnuts are rich in alpha-linolenic acid, an omega 3 fatty acid, and contain more polyphenols than any other nut. Polyphenols are critical for the brain to counteract oxidative stress and inflammation.

Crunchy Tahini Chocolate Grain Free Granola

When I first changed my eating habits, I did a cupboard clean out of all things processed. This meant that all the store-bought cereals had to go. Cereal with milk is easy and quick and I really missed having cold cereal for breakfast. Then I started making my own granola. When I want to keep my carbohydrates low, I eat this grain-free version. It's so full of good stuff that you'll never miss the oats.

Makes 4 cups (1000 ml)

- ¼ cup (60 ml) creamy tahini
- 1 tablespoon (15 ml) liquid coconut oil
- 1 teaspoon (5 ml) pure vanilla extract
- 1 cup (250 ml) raw cashews
- 1 cup (250 ml) raw pecans
- 1 cup (250 ml) raw almonds
- 1 teaspoon (5 ml) cinnamon
- ¼ teaspoon (1 ml) flaxseed
- ¾ cup (175 ml) unsweetened coconut flakes
- ⅓ cup (43 g) dairy free dark chocolate, chopped

Preheat oven to 300°F (149°C). Line a baking sheet with parchment paper.

Combine tahini, coconut oil, vanilla, and cinnamon in a medium saucepan and cook under low heat until melted and well combined. Set aside.

Combine the cashews, pecans, and almonds in a food processor and pulse briefly a few times to break them up into smaller pieces. (Do not over blend.) Transfer the nuts to a large bowl and add the flaxseed and coconut flakes. Pour the tahini mixture into the bowl and mix well. The dry ingredients should be evenly coated.

Transfer the granola to the prepared baking sheet and press it down firmly to form a rectangle. Bake, shaking the baking sheet gently every 10 minutes (not too hard or the clusters will break) until the granola is golden brown, 35 to 40 minutes.

Let the granola cool completely, then add the chopped dark chocolate and break up any large clusters. Granola will keep in the fridge for up to 2 weeks or in the freezer for several months.

Nesta's Almond Shake

This is a recipe my yoga teacher presented to us as a way to start our day and balance our doshas (constitution). We were learning about Ayurvedic medicine and the digestive system. This is simple to make and an alternative to a fruit smoothie.

Makes 1 serving

- 1 cup (250 ml) boiled organic milk or milk substitute
- 5 almonds soaked overnight and peeled
- 1 fig
- 4 dates
- Cinnamon, cardamom, and saffron to taste

Place all ingredients in the blender and blend until smooth. Pour into a mug.

Susanne's Tip: When cutting parchment paper to fit into a pan: Place the pan bottom-down on the paper. Use a pen or pencil to trace around the bottom and then cut with scissors. It will fit perfectly into the pan. Use a basting brush or tissue to spread a very thin layer of oil on the bottom of the pan to keep the paper in place.

Banana and Blueberry Loaf

This loaf is moist, delicious, and keto friendly. The first time I made it, I just greased the pan and cooked it in a toaster oven. The bottom stuck to the pan. Now I use parchment paper and grease the paper well. Use fresh, not frozen, blueberries as the frozen ones make the loaf soggy. Whenever I use almond meal or flour in a recipe, I always use fresh fruit.

Makes 1 loaf

- 3 tablespoons (45 ml) coconut oil or melted butter, plus extra for greasing the pan
- 3 very ripe bananas, peeled
- 3 free-range eggs
- 3 tablespoons (45 ml) maple syrup or sugar substitute
- 1 ½ cups plus 2 tablespoons (180 g) almond flour
- 1 teaspoon (5 ml) baking powder
- ½ teaspoon (2.5 ml) cinnamon
- ½ to 1 cup (125 to 250 ml) fresh blueberries
- If using stevia or other sugar substitute, add ½ teaspoon (2.5 ml) vanilla

---

Preheat the oven to 350°F (180°C).

Grease a 450 g (1 lb) loaf tin with coconut oil and line it with parchment paper. Melt the coconut oil/butter in a pan. In a mixing bowl using a fork, mash the bananas until smooth. Add the eggs, pour in the coconut oil, maple syrup, and vanilla extract (if using) and mix until combined.

Whisk in the almond flour, cinnamon, and baking powder until well combined. Finally, fold in the blueberries.

Pour the mixture into the lined tin, and bake for 50 to 60 minutes or until cooked through.

Chai Chia Breakfast

This is a simple make-ahead breakfast full of protein and healthy spices. If you're bored of the traditional breakfast fare, this adds some variety to your breakfast choices. It's important to eat a wide spectrum of foods to avoid developing food sensitivities. Experiment with your spices. How about adding some cocoa or turmeric?

Makes 2 servings

- 1 cup (250 ml) coconut milk (almond or macadamia also work)
- ¼ cup (60 ml) chia seeds
- ¾ teaspoon (4 ml) chai spice blend
- ¼ teaspoon (1 ml) vanilla extract
- ¼ teaspoon (1 ml) sweetener of your choice, stevia, monk fruit, honey, or maple syrup
- Chopped nuts such as almonds, pecans or walnuts as topping

The Chai Spice Blend:

This makes more than required for one recipe but keeps in a stored container to use repeatedly.

- 2 teaspoons (10 ml) ground cinnamon
- 2 teaspoons (10 ml) ground cardamom
- 1 teaspoon (5 ml) ground ginger
- 1 teaspoon (5 ml) ground cloves
- 1 teaspoon (5 ml) ground allspice

Stir the milk, chia seeds, ¾ teaspoon (4 ml) of spice blend, vanilla, and sweetener together in a bowl. You can also place in a blender and mix if you want a really smooth pudding. Divide the mixture evenly between two small jars. Refrigerate overnight to thicken.

Add the toppings when you're ready to eat.

Spiced Roasted Pumpkin Seeds

Pumpkin seeds are full of healthy nutrients but are most known for possessing zinc, which is an important neurotransmitter for making hormones like serotonin and dopamine. Zinc is a key player in the joy factor. I love these spicy seeds in salads, soups, over vegetables, or in my yogurt. They add a little crunch to the smoother, plainer foods you eat.

Makes 3 cups (750 ml)

- 3 tablespoons (45 ml) honey
- 1 tablespoon (15 ml) plus 1 teaspoon (5 ml) olive oil
- 1 ¼ teaspoon (6 ml) cinnamon
- ¾ teaspoon (4 ml) turmeric
- 1 teaspoon (5 ml) sea salt
- 2 cups (500 ml) raw, shelled pumpkin seeds

Heat oven to 325°F (163°C).

Line an 11 x 17 (28 x 43 cm) baking sheet with parchment paper. In a small saucepan over medium heat, heat honey and oil until bubbling. Remove from heat and whisk in cinnamon, turmeric, and salt, then pumpkin seeds until very well coated.

Spread seeds on a prepared baking sheet in an even layer. Bake for 20 minutes, stirring every 5 to 10 minutes, until seeds are golden brown and honey is caramelized. Remove from the oven, stir and cool completely at room temperature. Break up any clumps.

Pumpkin Seed Hummus

I love hummus with fresh vegetables and it's exciting that there are so many options when making it. Try this great alternative that has both chickpeas and pumpkin seeds. Chickpeas, also called garbanzo beans, are high in protein and fiber. They improve digestion, help keep your blood sugar low, and are packed with nutrients. Bonus: they're super cheap!

Makes 2 cups (500 ml)

- ½ cup (125 ml) roasted, salted pumpkin seeds, plus more for garnish
- 1 (15 ounces, 425 g) can chickpeas, drained and restrained
- 2 to 3 cloves garlic, chopped
- 2 tablespoons (30 ml) lemon juice
- 1 teaspoon (5 ml) ground cumin
- ¼ teaspoon (1 ml) ground cayenne
- ½ teaspoon (2.5 ml) sweet paprika
- 2 tablespoons (30 ml) extra virgin olive oil, plus more for garnish
- 3 to 4 tablespoons (60 ml) water
- ¼ teaspoon (1 ml) sea salt
- ¼ teaspoon (1 ml) black pepper
- **Smoked paprika for garnish (optional)**

In a food processor or blender, combine the pumpkin seeds, chickpeas, garlic, lemon juice, cumin, cayenne, sweet paprika, oil, salt and pepper.

Process until smooth, scraping down the sides as needed. If too thick, add 1 tablespoon (15 ml) of water at a time until you reach desired consistency.

Transfer to a serving bowl and garnish with a drizzle of olive oil, a dusting of smoked paprika, and toasted pumpkin seeds.

Did you know that hummus is the Arabic word for chickpea?

Almond Meal Pizza Crust

It's super hard to find a gluten free pizza crust that's healthy AND tasty. Most contain corn, soy, vegetable oils, and preservatives. Read the labels: just because it's gluten-free doesn't mean it's healthy. Here's an easy, homemade alternative. It doesn't have the traditional doughy taste of pizza parlour crusts but still tastes delicious with your favourite toppings.

Makes 1 pizza crust

- 2 cups (500 ml) almond meal
- 2 medium-sized eggs
- ¼ teaspoon (1 ml) baking soda
- 3 tablespoons (45 ml) olive oil

Preheat the oven to 350°F (177°C).

Lightly grease a pizza sheet with olive oil.

Place all ingredients in a bowl and using a spoon mix together until the dough becomes very thick. Form into a ball. Place the ball of dough in the center of the pizza pan. Place a piece of plastic over the dough, and flatten and push the dough outward toward the edges of the pizza pan. Make the dough as thin as possible. Bake for 20 minutes.

Add toppings and heat for another 25 to 30 minutes or until toppings are heated through and cheese is bubbly.

Walnut, Arugula, and Lemon Pasta

I love cooked greens for a change of pace and this dish satisfies my cravings for pasta. Walnuts are full of nutrients and are a good source of omega 3s. Homemade bone broth adds to the nutritional value of this dish.

Serves 4

- ¼ cup (125 ml) extra virgin olive oil
- 2 cloves garlic, minced
- ⅔ cup (170 g) walnuts
- 1 ½ teaspoon (7.5 ml) salt
- 12 oz. (340 g) gluten free pasta
- 3 cups (750 ml) baby arugula leaves, stems intact or 1 bunch mature with stems and midribs removed, leaves coarsely chopped
- 2 tablespoons (30 ml) chicken or vegetable broth
- 1 teaspoon (5 ml) freshly cracked pepper
- 2 tablespoons (30 ml) lemon zest
- ¼ cup (60 ml) parmesan, pecorino cheese, or brewer's yeast
- 2 tablespoons (30 ml) of fresh lemon juice
- 1 lemon, cut into wedges

In a small frying pan over medium, heat the olive oil. Add the garlic, sautéing until it's lightly golden, about 3 minutes. Remove from heat.

Place the walnuts on a cookie tray and toast in the oven at 350°F (177°C). This will only take 3 to 5 minutes. Remove from heat, cool, and chop. Set aside.

In a large pot, boil water and add 1 teaspoon (5 ml) salt. Cook pasta. Drain immediately.

Put the arugula in the bottom of a large bowl and add the hot pasta. Add the chicken broth to the skillet with garlic and heat over medium heat for 1 minute, then pour it over the pasta, tossing to coat. Stir in the remaining salt, pepper, lemon zest, half of the cheese, and all but 1 tablespoon (15 ml) of the walnuts. Add the lemon juice and combine.

Garnish with remaining cheese and walnuts and serve with lemon wedges.

Banana-Coconut Baked Oatmeal

Baked oatmeal is a trendy food and there are a million different recipes you can try, but I found this version to be a hit. It's great served for brunch or a small gathering. Pair it with one of the egg dishes above and you've covered all your bases. Buy gluten free sprouted oats if you can for better digestion but remember that they're high in carbs – moderation is the key. (It's so delicious you might want to eat the whole thing yourself!)

Serves 4–5

Wet:
- ⅔ cup (160 ml) light coconut milk
- ⅓ cup (80 ml) pure maple syrup plus 2 tablespoons (30 ml) unsalted butter, melted
- 1 ripe banana
- 1 large egg

Dry:
- 2 cups (500 ml) old-fashioned oats
- 1 teaspoon (5 ml) aluminum-free baking powder
- ½ teaspoon (2.5 ml) cinnamon
- ½ teaspoon (2.5 ml) salt
- ⅛ teaspoon (0.5 ml) cardamom
- Grate fresh whole nutmeg

Garnish (optional)
- Large flaked unsweetened coconut
- Plain whole milk yogurt
- Banana slices
- Chopped nuts
- Pumpkin seeds
- Hemp seeds
- Bee pollen

Preheat the oven to 375°F (190°C).

In a 12 x 10-inch (25 x 25 cm) enamel baking dish (or similar-sized glass or ceramic dish), stir together all of the dry ingredients inside the pan. Set aside.

In a blender, combine all of the wet ingredients, including the melted butter, and blend on medium-low until just combined. Pour the wet mixture over the dry mixture in the baking dish, and stir well to combine. Wipe down the exposed sides of the pan, if needed. Bake for 13 to 15 minutes or until a light press in the centre bounces back. Serve warm. Add garnishes as desired.

Crunchy Apple Salad with Honey Walnut Dressing

This salad is more like a slaw. It's a powerhouse of prebiotic ingredients and nutrients. Even the dressing is rich in vitamins and minerals from the vegetables and greens. It's one of the nicest looking salads you can make. Great for brightening up the plate!

Serves 6

For the dressing:

- ¾ cup (175 ml) walnuts
- ¼ cup (60 ml) fresh lemon juice
- ¼ cup (60 ml) water
- 3 tablespoons (45 ml) honey
- 1 ½ tablespoons (22.5 ml) pomegranate vinegar
- ¼ teaspoon (1 ml) ground cinnamon
- ¼ teaspoon (1 ml) sea salt, or to taste
- Freshly ground black pepper, to taste

For the salad:

- 8 cups (2 litres) shredded crunchy vegetables such as kale, red cabbage, Brusselss sprouts, carrots, and broccoli (or broccoli slaw mix)
- ½ cup (125 ml) thinly sliced scallions
- ½ cup (125 ml) pomegranate seeds
- ½ cup (125 ml) chopped cilantro
- 2 sweet apples, such as Gala, cored and cut into thin matchsticks

---

Prepare the dressing:

Heat a dry skillet over medium-low heat. Toast the walnuts in a single layer, stirring occasionally, until lightly browned and fragrant, about 5 minutes. Transfer to a small food processor or blender. Add the remaining dressing ingredients and process until smooth and creamy. Adjust seasonings to taste. Refrigerate until ready to toss salad.

Prepare the salad:

Toss the vegetables, scallions, pomegranate seeds, cilantro, and apples in a large bowl. Drizzle with the dressing and toss until evenly coated.

Roasted Curried Chickpeas and Almonds

Roasted chickpeas are a popular food trend. In this recipe I threw in some almonds, a few spices and voila! An easy snack or side dish!

Makes 1 cup (250 ml)

- ½ cup (125 ml) canned chickpeas, drained and rinsed
- ½ cup (125 ml) whole raw almonds
- 2 teaspoons (10 ml) coconut oil
- 1 ½ teaspoon (7.5 ml) curry powder
- ½ teaspoon (2.5 ml) lime zest

Arrange chickpeas and almonds in a single layer on a parchment lined baking sheet; roast at 375°F (190°C) until golden brown, 15 to 18 minutes (stirring about midway). Sprinkle with lime zest.

Wasabi Peanuts

Store bought peanuts and nuts tend to be coated in sugars, salts, and vegetable oils, not to mention flour. Making your own is fun and much healthier. Peanuts are a good source of protein.

Makes 1 cup (250 ml)

- 1 egg white
- ¾ cup (175 ml) raw shelled peanuts
- 1 tablespoon (15 ml) plus 1 teaspoon (5 ml) wasabi powder
- ¼ teaspoon (1 ml) salt
- ⅛ teaspoon (0.5 ml) cayenne pepper

In a medium bowl, whisk the egg white until foamy. Stir in peanuts until coated well.

In a small bowl, whisk the wasabi powder, salt, and cayenne pepper. Stir into nut mix until coated. Arrange in 1 layer on a parchment lined baking sheet; roast at 300°F (177°C) until golden brown, 25 to 30 minutes (tossing halfway through the cooking time).

Pecan Nut Butter

I love pecans raw and plain, but add a little cinnamon and salt and they reach a whole new level of deliciousness. Blend them into a butter and serve them on toast, crackers, or slices of fruit.

Makes 1 cup (250 ml)

- **1-pound (454 g) raw pecans (preferably organic)**
- **2 teaspoons (10 ml) ground cinnamon, or more to taste**
- **Pinch of Himalayan pink salt (or a good quality sea salt)**

Preheat the oven to 350°F (177°C).

Spread the pecans on a baking sheet and roast for 7 to 10 minutes, watching them carefully so they don't burn. You want a slight toast; if they overcook, they'll get bitter. When done, remove from the oven, transfer to a plate, and let cool.

Add the nuts to a food processor and process on high power. Depending on your food processor, you may have to stop several times and scrape down the sides. After about 2 minutes on high power, they start releasing their oils. Continue processing until you get that butter-like consistency. Mine takes about 5 minutes.

Add the cinnamon and salt, making sure you don't add too much salt. Add just a little, mix again and taste, and if you feel it needs more, you can add it afterward, but you can't take it back if you add too much. You can add more cinnamon if you'd like. Once done, scrape into a glass jar, let cool, cover with a tight-fitting lid, and store in the fridge for a few weeks.

Green with Envy: Greens and Leafy Veggies

Leafy green vegetables are packed with essential nutrients, water, and fiber and are low in calories. They can be found year-round, and organic greens are readily available in most grocery stores. In terms of brain health, eating greens is essential. They're anti-aging, anti-inflammatory, and help prevent plaque build up in the brain. Greens consumption also lifts your spirits and helps eliminates depression.

It's important to find some greens that you love and eat them as often as you can. If you get bored, it's time to be adventurous in terms of trying new vegetables or combinations of greens. There are lots of options to choose from in your local store or farmers' market, and growing your own is easy and economical. There are Bok choy, Napa cabbage, kale, collard, Swiss chard, arugula, endive, chicory, mesclun, and wild greens, just to name a few. I prefer microgreens, which are immature greens that typically measure between 1 and 3 inches (2.5 - 7.5 cm). They're a powerhouse of nutrients containing up to 40 times more the nutrients of the mature plant.

Spinach, Swiss chard, and beet greens should be eaten in moderation because they contain oxalic acid, which causes kidney and gallbladder stones. They also deplete calcium from bones and teeth, which can lead to osteoporosis. Cooking your greens with a healthy fat will neutralize the effect of this acid.

You can eat your greens raw or cooked. To best absorb their nutrients, they must be eaten with a healthy fat such as olive oil. Without the oil, you won't benefit from taking the greens.

Green Vitamin Packed Juice

Only make this juice if you can find organic celery and grapes. These two items make the top of the "dirty dozen" list of pesticide-laden foods. Leave the skin on the cucumber because it's packed with biotin, which is necessary for healthy bones and healthy brain function. This juice is delicious. I even serve it as a cocktail with brunch.

Serves 2

- ½ large cucumber
- 3 stalks of celery
- 2-3 large broccoli florets
- 10-12 green grapes
- 2-3 stems kale or Swiss chard
- 1 Gala apple
- ½ cup (125 ml) or a handful of parsley

Wash all your produce. Put all your vegetables and fruit through your juicer. Drink immediately for maximum nutritional value.

Susanne's Tip: Rinsing produce in apple cider vinegar helps to clean and purify them before use.

Basic Salad Dressing

As mentioned previously, we need to serve our greens with some healthy oil. Store bought dressings are chemicals in a bottle. Once you start making your own dressings you'll never go back to the bottle, but be aware that homemade dressing doesn't last as long as store bought. Store in the fridge from anywhere from 3 to 4 days if you're adding fresh spices or nuts and seeds, and up to 2 weeks if using only dried spices.

- 1 - part vinegar
- 2 - parts oil

Pour vinegar into a container. Add oil. Mix.

This is the basic recipe. If you choose ½ cup (125 ml) vinegar, you would add 1 cup (250 ml) oil. However, I often use an equal amount of vinegar and oil, so a 1:1 ratio. Many chefs say the best ratio is 1:3 but I find it a bit heavy on the oil. There are lots of options for both oils and vinegars. Try using different olive, avocado, coconut, flax seed, or almond oils. Some vinegars to experiment with include balsamic, red wine, apple cider vinegar, or pomegranate. Some fruit vinegars are filled with added sugar so please read the label before purchasing.

A little sweetener mellows the vinegar and improves flavour. Try a bit of raw honey, maple syrup, or some fruit juice. Avoid white sugar or cane juice. Spices take your salad dressing to a new level. The options are endless: basil, rosemary, oregano, turmeric, ginger, etc.

A dab of Dijon mustard also adds some depth to the dressing. Experiment with the amount and try other types of mustards.

I make my dressing in a large enough quantity to last a week and usually have at least 2 different types on hand.

Did you know that eating foods raw (fruit and veggies) magnifies their benefits and improves your mental health?

Tamari Dressing

If you're looking for a salad dressing that's a little bit different, try this recipe. Tamari is gluten free soy sauce that is less salty and more flavourful.

- 1 - part Tamari
- 1 - part vinegar
- 2 - parts oil

Mix together in a jar and shake. Add spices to taste and some salt and pepper if desired.

Store in the fridge for up to 3 days. Shake just before serving.

Layered Jar Salads

I love having dinner parties and presenting my food in new and exciting ways. When the mason jar craze began, I had a "girls' luncheon" and served these salads in a jar. They were a huge hit. You can eat the salad right out of the jar or empty it onto your plate.

Makes 4 servings

Dressing:

- ¼ cup (60 ml) olive oil
- 2 tablespoons (30 ml) balsamic vinegar
- 1 garlic clove, minced
- ½ teaspoon (2.5 ml) honey
- ¼ teaspoon (1 ml) salt
- ⅛ teaspoon (0.5 ml) black pepper

Salad Layers:

- ½ cup (125 ml) diced red onion
- 1 can (15 oz./450 grams) cannellini beans, drained and rinsed
- 1 tomato, diced, or equivalent in grape tomatoes
- 8 cups (2 litre) fresh arugula or other greens
- ½ cup (125 ml) freshly grated parmesan cheese or other cheese

---

General instructions for jar salads: To make layered salads, place the dressing on the bottom of jar then add one or two "wet" ingredients for the next layer (beans, chickpeas, tomatoes, or grains). Add the greens and cheese. Shake together before serving. Alternatively, you could opt to serve the dressing when serving.

Make the dressing by mixing ingredients together in a small jar. Divide the dressing between four jars.

Add these ingredients in this order: onions, beans, tomatoes, arugula, and preferred cheese.

Store in the fridge for up to 3 days. Shake just before serving.

Did you know that you should make your salad dressing ahead of time so the flavours mellow and develop taste?

Cobb Salad

This is a slightly different take on an old classic and just as delicious as the original version. I love the crunch that the nuts contribute and the bit of sweetness provided by the fruit. You can mix it up using any combination of nuts, seeds, fruits, and greens. This salad has it all: protein, greens, fruit, vegetables, and healthy fats.

Makes 4 or 5 servings

- 1 container or head of lettuce (spring mix, Boston, spinach, etc.)
- 4 eggs, hard-boiled
- 2 avocados, pitted, peeled, and diced
- 2 tomatoes (or equivalent amount in grape tomatoes)
- 1 apple or pear, cored and diced
- ½ to 1 cup (125 to 250 ml) chopped nuts (pecans, walnuts, etc.)
- 3 to 4 ounces (175 to 250 ml) crumbled or chopped goat feta cheese

Dressing:
- ¼ cup (60 ml) olive oil
- 1 tablespoon (15 ml) red wine vinegar
- 1 teaspoon (5 ml) honey
- ½ teaspoon (2.5 ml) Dijon mustard
- 1 clove garlic, minced
- ¼ teaspoon (1 ml) salt
- Ground pepper to taste

Place the lettuce on one large platter or individual plates. Then arrange the eggs, avocados, tomatoes, apple, and cheese in rows over the lettuce.

Make the dressing by mixing all ingredients together. Pour over salad and serve.

Creamy Artichoke Dip

Artichokes are somewhat of a super food. They're packed with nutrients, high in fiber, and have been used for centuries for their medicinal properties. In fact, artichoke is an increasingly popular supplement. They are not actually a vegetable but a type of thistle. Their cholesterol lowering effects, ability to lower blood sugar, and contribution to good gut health make them a perfect food to include in your eat for joy food plan.

Serves 4

- Two 10 oz. (280 g) jars artichokes in water and salt
- 6 tablespoons (90 ml) finely chopped red onion, previously soaked in ice water for 10 minutes
- 6 tablespoons (90 ml) avocado mayonnaise
- 2 small cloves garlic
- ½ teaspoon (2.5 ml) lemon juice
- 4 anchovy fillets, finely chopped
- 1 cup (250 ml) spinach, chopped (optional)
- 2 tablespoons (30 ml) extra-virgin olive oil
- Sea salt flakes and pepper to taste (if necessary)
- Smoked sea salt

Rinse and drain the artichokes well and squeeze them in a paper towel to take out as much of the water as possible. Add the artichokes to a food processor and process until well chopped.

Add the onion, mayonnaise, garlic, lemon juice, and anchovies, and mix again. Drizzle in the olive oil through the feed tube while the processor is running. Taste for salt and pepper (the anchovies and mayo might have enough salt already). Add if needed.

Sprinkle with smoked sea salt and serve with crackers or vegetable sticks.

Crazy about Cruciferous Vegetables

Cruciferous vegetables have properties said to prevent or delay cognitive decline in the aged. They benefit our memory centers and protect the brain from toxins. They're also good for your heart and blood vessels, both of which are needed for healthy blood flow to the brain. They're full of fiber so they aid in healthy digestion. You really can't go wrong eating these powerhouses from the vegetable kingdom.

The family of vegetables known as cruciferous include arugula, Bok choy, broccoli, broccoli rabe, Brussels sprouts, cabbage, cauliflower, collard greens, daikon, horseradish, kale, kohlrabi, mustard, radish, rutabaga, turnips, wasabi, and watercress.

Arugula Salad with Roasted Sweet Potatoes, Caramelized Onions, and Steak

Arugula is actually a cruciferous vegetable and not a green. No matter what we label it, it's delicious and slightly peppery. I buy baby arugula for its slightly milder taste, softer stems, and higher nutrient value. This dish combines so many great foods in one bowl.

Serves 4

- 8 tablespoons (120 ml) avocado oil
- 1 red onion, halved and sliced into thin half moons
- 1 sweet potato, scrubbed and cut into 1 ½ inch (3.81 cm) cubes
- 2 teaspoons (10 ml) balsamic vinegar
- Fine sea salt and freshly ground black pepper
- 1 tablespoon (15 ml) ghee or butter
- 2 pounds (.907 kg) of steak, cut into 2 or 3 pieces
- 2 tablespoons (30 ml) red wine vinegar
- 1 teaspoon (5 ml) Dijon mustard
- 10 cups (2.5 litres) baby arugula
- 1-pint grape tomatoes, mix of red and yellow, halved

Heat 2 tablespoons (30 ml) of the oil in a large skillet over medium heat. Add the onion and sauté until soft, about 7 minutes. Add the sweet potato and balsamic vinegar and sauté for 10 minutes, until the sweet potatoes are crisp-tender. Season with salt and pepper to taste, then transfer the mixture to a plate to cool.

Wipe the pan clean, return it to medium-high heat, and add the ghee. Season the steaks generously with salt and pepper, add them to the pan and cook for 5 minutes per side, until a thermometer inserted into the thickest part of each steak reads 140°F (60°C) for medium rare. Transfer the steaks to a cutting board and let them rest for 5 minutes.

In a large bowl, whisk together the remaining 6 tablespoons (90 ml) of oil, vinegar, mustard, ¼ teaspoon (1.25 ml) salt, and a pinch of pepper. Add the arugula and tomatoes to the bowl and toss gently to combine.

Thinly slice the steaks diagonally against the grain. Divide the salad mixture among the plates and top each with some of the caramelized onion and sweet potato mixture and a few slices of steak. Serve immediately.

Did you know that you should always let your meats "rest" before slicing them? Place them on a cutting board and cover with tinfoil to let the meat absorb the juices so it remains juicy. Five to 10 minutes should be sufficient for smaller cuts, while 15 or 20 minutes may be needed for larger servings like a turkey.

Low Carb Cabbage Rolls (Vegetarian or Meat)

Makes 6 servings

- 1 head green cabbage
- 1 small cauliflower (or premade cauliflower rice in a package)
- 2 tablespoons (30 ml) avocado oil
- ¼ cup (60 ml) onion, diced
- 1 cup (250 ml) bone or vegetable broth
- 1 large egg
- 1 can (14.5 ounces, 411 grams) diced tomatoes, drained and liquid reserved
- 1 teaspoon (5 ml) kosher salt
- ½ teaspoon (2.5 ml) black pepper
- 1-pound (450 g) ground beef or mushrooms, cut into small pieces

---

Remove outer leaves of the cabbage. Bring a large pot of water to a boil and drop in the cabbage leaves. Boil for 2 minutes or until softened, then remove carefully and dry on a kitchen towel.

Use a food processor with a shredding grate to grate the cauliflower florets. Measure 2 cups (500 ml). Save any leftovers for another recipe. Or use packaged cauliflower rice.

In a medium skillet, heat the oil over medium heat. Add the onion and sauté 2 minutes. Add the cauliflower and half (1/2 cup/120 ml) of the broth. Cook, stirring occasionally for about 5 minutes until cauliflower is cooked but still firm. Remove from the heat and allow to cool slightly.

In a large bowl, lightly beat the eggs. Mix in drained tomatoes, salt and pepper, ground beef or mushrooms and mix well. Add the cauliflower mixture and stir to combine.

Divide the mixture evenly among the leaves, placing the filling in the center of each. Fold the sides and roll each one up tightly. Secure with a toothpick.

Mix reserved tomato juice with remaining ½ cup (125 ml) broth.

Cook in a skillet or in a slow cooker.

In a skillet on the stovetop, place the rolls in a single layer. Pour the broth mixture over them and cover. Heat over medium heat until liquid boils, then reduce the heat to low. Cook about 40 minutes, occasionally spooning liquid over rolls.

In a slow cooker, place rolls in a small slow cooker. Pour liquid over, cover, and cook on low for 7 to 8 hours.

If using a thermometer to check the cabbage rolls, the internal temperature should reach 160° F (70° C).

Whole Baked Cauliflower with Tahini Sauce and Slivered Almonds

I am a huge cauliflower fan. It's so versatile and it's similar to tofu in that it takes on the taste of whatever spices or sauces it's cooked in. This recipe is one you must try! Feel free to substitute the almonds with pistachios and pomegranate seeds.

Serves 4 to 6

- 1 whole cauliflower
- ½ cup (125 ml) olive oil
- 2 teaspoons (10 ml) paprika
- 1 teaspoon (5 ml) garlic powder
- 1 teaspoon (5 ml) onion powder
- 1 teaspoon (5 ml) oregano
- ½ teaspoon (2.5 ml) allspice
- ½ teaspoon (2.5 ml) salt
- ¼ teaspoon (1.5 ml) black pepper

Tahini Sauce:

- 1 cup (250 ml) tahini
- ½ cup (125 ml) fresh lemon
- 1 clove garlic, crushed
- 6-8 tablespoons (90 to 120 ml) water
- Salt and pepper, to taste
- Slivered almonds, toasted

Preheat the oven to 400°F (204°C).

Line a baking dish with parchment. Wash cauliflower, remove leaves, and slice the bottom so it sits evenly in the dish.

In a bowl, combine oil and spices. Flip the cauliflower and place a few tablespoons of the mixture inside the cavity. Turn the cauliflower upright in the dish and rub the rest of the spice mixture over the cauliflower.

Roast for 45 minutes or until tender. Cooking time depends on the size of the cauliflower.

Prepare the sauce by mixing tahini, lemon juice, and garlic. It will be very thick. Slowly mix in water until the sauce loosens to pouring consistency. Season with salt and pepper. Serve the cauliflower with Tahini sauce and sliced almonds.

Honey-Mustard Glazed Brussels Sprouts

I love adding honey and mustard to salmon or chicken, but what about adding it to your veggies? The combination of these little cabbages with the honey-mustard sauce is inspired.

Serves 6

- 2 tablespoons (30 ml) Dijon mustard
- 2 tablespoons (30 ml) raw honey
- Salt and pepper
- 1 ¼ pounds (.576 kg) Brussels sprouts
- 3 tablespoons (45 ml) olive oil

Preheat the oven to 400°F (204°C).

Put a rimmed baking pan in the oven for 10 minutes.

In a small bowl, mix mustard and honey, and season with salt and pepper.

Trim the bottoms off the Brussels sprouts, and slice in half from top to bottom. Put them in a large bowl, add oil, salt and pepper, and toss to coat. Put the Brussels sprouts on the hot cookie sheet, cut side down in an even layer. Cook undisturbed, until the sprouts brown, about 10 minutes. Turn the sprouts and continue roasting for 10 minutes.

Remove the baking sheet from the oven, add the honey mustard, and toss to coat. Return to the oven, and cook for 5 more minutes or until cooked through.

Susanne's Tip: Preheating your baking sheets in the oven will ensure a faster and more even roast on your veggies.

Roasted Coleslaw

I love cooked cabbage and I love coleslaw. Mixing these two recipes together is sheer brilliance. Cruciferous vegetables, such as cabbage, are super nutritious and loaded with antioxidants. They're a good prebiotic that aid in healing our gut and they're a staple of the cancer prevention diet. Serve this coleslaw with fish, salmon, or meat or use as a topping for your salad greens. Double the recipe to serve a crowd.

Serves 4 to 6 servings

- 1 head of green cabbage, chopped or shredded
- 1 to 2 carrots, chopped or shredded
- 1 tablespoon (15 ml) coconut or avocado oil
- ¼ teaspoon (1 ml) Himalayan pink salt
- Ground pepper to taste
- 1 clove garlic, minced
- 1 - 2 scallions, green and white parts sliced for garnish

Dressing:

- 4 tablespoons (60 ml) apple cider vinegar
- 2 tablespoons (30 ml) sesame oil
- 1 tablespoon (15 ml) grated fresh ginger
- ¼ teaspoon (1 ml) red pepper flakes

Preheat the oven to 425°F (218°C).

On a baking sheet, toss the carrots and cabbage with the coconut oil, salt, and a few grinds of fresh pepper. Spread evenly on the cookie sheet and roast in the oven for 20 to 30 minutes. Stir every 10 minutes. The cabbage should be golden brown and tender. Add the garlic in the last 5 minutes of cooking.

To make the dressing, whisk all ingredients in a small bowl.

Transfer cabbage to a bowl and toss with 1 to 2 tablespoons (15 to 30 ml) of the dressing.

Season to taste and garnish with scallions.

Did you know that onions usually need to be "sweated" in the pan before other ingredients are added? This process removes their bitterness and keeps it from bleeding into the other ingredients.

Raving about Root Vegetables

Root vegetables are packed with antioxidants and fiber, but they're high in carbohydrates. In fact, some nutritionists consider them more like a grain than a vegetable. Even though they are low in calories, it's wise when planning your meals for the day to consider your daily carbohydrate load. Don't eat all your root vegetables at the same time and eat a wider variety of them to get a selection of nutrients.

Some plants that grow underground are roots such as beets, carrots, and parsnips, others are bulbous growths like fennel and onions, and still others are tubers and tuberous roots like sweet potatoes, potatoes, yams, and yucca. There are rhizomes like ginger and turmeric.

I believe that root vegetables are some of the most nutritious foods you can eat and they're also incredibly versatile: You can eat them boiled, mashed, baked, or roasted with olive oil, or you can use them to make delicious and hearty soups or casseroles.

Spiced Carrot Hummus

Harissa paste, a North African spicy red sauce, makes the hummus in this recipe full of flavour. Serve with raw vegetables or gluten free crackers. If you want to make your own harissa paste, the Minimalist Baker has a great DIY recipe online. Your favourite purchased hot sauce will work just as well.

Serves 4 to 6

- 2 small to medium carrots, coarsely grated
- 1 14 oz. (400 g) tin chickpeas, drained and rinsed
- 2 garlic cloves, crushed
- Juice of ½ a lemon
- 2/3 cup (150 ml) olive oil
- 2 teaspoons (10 ml) tahini
- 2 teaspoons (10 ml) harissa paste (hot chili paste) or hot sauce

---

Place all the ingredients in a food processor with salt and pepper. Blend until smooth and creamy. Can be made 2 days ahead but does not freeze well.

Roasted Butternut Carrot Ginger Soup

I love to find different combinations of flavours to put in my soups, like pear and parsnip, or mushroom and spinach. This soup combines butternut squash, carrots, and ginger. It's loaded with potassium, vitamin C, and B6, and has 334% of your daily requirement of vitamin A just from the carrots. Ginger is anti-inflammatory and contains a healthy dose of magnesium. Turmeric and cayenne pepper are also anti-inflammatory.

Serves 4 to 6

- 1 whole butternut squash
- 8 carrots, peeled and cut into quarters
- 2 organic apples, peeled and cubed
- 1 small onion, cut into quarters
- 4 or 5 whole garlic cloves, chopped coarsely
- Fresh ginger, peeled and cut into bite sized pieces
- 4-6 cups (500-600 ml) vegetable broth
- 2 tablespoons (30 ml) avocado, olive, or coconut oil
- ½ teaspoon (2.5 ml) Himalayan salt
- ¼ teaspoon (1 ml) black pepper
- ½ to 1 teaspoon (2.5 to 5 ml) turmeric
- Pinch of cayenne pepper

Preheat the oven to 400°F (204°C).

In a large bowl, toss the squash, carrots, apple, onion, garlic, ginger, and salt and pepper with the oil. Place on a cookie sheet and bake for 40 to 45 minutes. Remove from the oven and let cool.

In a blender, add half the roasted veggies and half the broth. Blend until you have a thick puréed texture. Set aside and repeat the procedure with the remaining veggies and broth.

Pour all the puréed ingredients into a large saucepan, add turmeric and cayenne pepper and a pinch of salt (optional). Heat the soup on medium low for 12 to 15 minutes and serve.

Vegan Sweet Potato Gnocchi

One thing I hear from clients is that they miss the "comfort" foods they grew up eating, so I'm always looking for healthy and delicious takes on these recipes and this one hits the mark. Gnocchi is a comfort food usually made with white flour and potatoes but this one changes things up by substituting sweet potato and cassava flour and it's served with a creamy sauce. I make a batch of these delights and freeze them. They make a quick but impressive first course.

Serves 4

- 2 cups (500 ml) mashed sweet potato
- 1 ¼ cups (310 ml) flour, or gluten free 1-to-1 flour
- ⅛ cup (79 ml) olive oil, or coconut oil, or avocado oil
- 1 teaspoon (5 ml) sea salt

Garlic Sage Sauce

- 1 tablespoon (15 ml) olive oil
- 1 cup (250 ml) light coconut milk
- ¼ cup (59 ml) chopped sage
- 2 teaspoons (10 ml) minced garlic
- 2 teaspoons (10 ml) arrowroot powder
- 1 teaspoon (5 ml) sea salt

To make the gnocchi: Place mashed sweet potato in a large bowl. Add flour, sea salt, and oil to the bowl, and knead ingredients until they're a consistent dough. Make sure that all of the flour is absorbed. The dough will be ready when nothing is sticking to the bowl.

Flour a clear surface with extra flour and place the dough onto the floured surface. Use a knife to slice the dough in quarters.

Take one quarter and roll the sweet potato dough into a long rope about 1 inch (2.5 cm) thick. Slice in 1-inch sections with a pizza slicer or thin knife.

Tuck the edges so that they are more rounded and lightly flour. Place the ready-to-boil gnocchi onto a plate and repeat with the remaining quarters.

When you have shaped all the gnocchi, bring a large pot with 2 quarts (1.89 litres) of water and a pinch of sea salt to a boil.

When the water is boiling, add about ¼ of the gnocchi to the pot and give the water a swirl. Let the gnocchi cook until they start to rise to the top (about 1 to 2 minutes). When they've risen, remove them from the water, and repeat for the remaining gnocchi.

Once all the gnocchi are cooked, add 1 teaspoon (5 ml) olive oil to a large sauté pan and sauté the gnocchi until crispy. Turn off the heat and cover to keep warm.

To make the sauce: In a separate large sauté pan, heat the remaining oil on medium-high heat and add the minced garlic to the pan. Sauté until golden brown, then reduce the heat to medium and add the sage.

Sauté the garlic and sage together until fragrant, then add in the coconut milk, sea salt, and arrowroot powder.

Stir until the arrowroot powder is combined, and let the sauce cook on medium-low heat for 5 minutes, or until thickened.

Once the sauce is thickened, add the gnocchi to the pan and toss until coated.

Serve with fresh pepper.

Brunch Sweet Potatoes

This is a great recipe to serve a crowd for breakfast or brunch. It's easy and goes perfectly with an egg casserole and a fresh salad.

Serves 8

- 1 ¼ pounds (568 g) sweet potatoes
- 1 cup (250 ml) thinly sliced red onions
- 1 cup (250 ml) vegetable or bone broth, plus more if needed
- 2 teaspoons (10 ml) chopped fresh thyme or 1 teaspoon (5 ml) dried, divided
- 1 ¼ teaspoon (6 ml) chili powder, divided
- ½ teaspoon (2.5 ml) dried oregano
- ½ teaspoon (2.5 ml) garlic powder
- ¼ teaspoon (1 ml) fine sea salt
- ⅛ teaspoon (0.5 ml) freshly ground black pepper

Peel sweet potatoes and chop into ½ inch (1.25cm) chunks approximately 4 ½ cups (1125ml).

In a 12 in (30.5 cm) heavy bottomed skillet combine the sweet potatoes, onions, broth, 1 teaspoon (5 ml) fresh thyme (or ½ teaspoon (2.5 ml) dried), ¾ teaspoon (3.7 ml) chili powder, oregano, garlic powder, salt and pepper. Bring to a boil over high heat.

Reduce heat to medium-high. Cook, stirring frequently, until potatoes are tender and liquid is mostly evaporated, about 10 minutes. If liquid evaporates before potatoes are tender, add additional broth as needed.

Stir in remaining 1 teaspoon (5 ml) thyme and chili powder. Taste for seasoning, adding more salt or pepper as needed.

Serve warm.

No Tomato Pasta Sauce

Tomatoes are inflammatory for many people, especially if they're sensitive to the night shade vegetables. An alternative is this sauce made with sweet potatoes and carrots.

Makes 2 to 3 cups (500 to 750 ml)

- 2 medium sweet potatoes, peeled and chopped
- 6 large carrots
- 3 tablespoons (45 ml) water
- ½ cup (125 ml) broth, vegetable or bone broth
- 1 tablespoon (15 ml) olive oil
- 3 tablespoons (45 ml) milk, or non-dairy milk
- Pinch of ground nutmeg
- Salt and pepper to taste

Place sweet potatoes and carrots in a saucepan with a steamer until fork-tender, about 15 minutes. Place in a blender and purée with 3 tablespoons (45 ml) water until smooth. In a pot over medium heat, whisk purée for 5 minutes with broth, olive oil, milk, nutmeg, and salt and pepper.

Serve over pasta.

Sweet Potato Shepherd's Pie

I once picked up a prepared shepherd's pie at a grocery store for an easy supper. I started reading the list of ingredients and was shocked at all the preservatives and chemicals. How could such an easy recipe contain all these extra toxins? I put it back on the shelf and went home and made my own. This recipe is even healthier than the traditional with use of sweet potato and grass-fed beef.

4 servings

Topping:

- 5 small or 3 medium sweet potatoes, peeled and cut into chunks
- ½ teaspoon (2.5 ml) ground cinnamon
- ¼ teaspoon (1 ml) ground nutmeg
- ½ teaspoon (2.5 ml) garlic powder
- 2 tablespoons (30 ml) organic ghee or butter
- ½ cup (118 ml) non-dairy milk of your choice

Bottom:

- 1.1 pounds (0.5 kg) grass-fed ground beef, chicken, or turkey
- 2 small onions, finely chopped
- 2 cups (500 ml) carrots, finely chopped
- 2 cups (500 ml) frozen peas, thawed
- 1 sweet yellow pepper, finely chopped
- 1 tablespoon (15 ml) fresh thyme, chopped
- 1 tablespoon (15 ml) fresh rosemary, chopped
- 2 garlic cloves, finely chopped
- 1 can (5.5 oz./156 ml) tomato paste
- ¾ cup (175 ml) chicken or veggie stock

Preheat oven to 350°F (180°C).

Fill a large pot with water. Place sweet potatoes in water and bring to a boil. Cook for 12 minutes or until potatoes are fork tender.

Transfer potatoes to a food processor if you want the top nice and smooth or use an immersion blender to purée the potatoes. A potato masher also works. Add cinnamon, nutmeg, garlic powder, ghee or butter, and non-dairy milk of your choice to the potatoes. Set aside.

In a large frying pan on medium heat, sauté the ground meat until no longer pink. Once done, set aside on a plate. In the same pan with heat on medium, cook onions. After a few minutes, add carrots and cook for 5 more minutes. Next, add the yellow pepper and cook for 2 more minutes and then add the thawed peas, garlic, fresh herbs, and finally the ground meat. Mix until combined. Add the tomato paste and veggie stock, mixing them well into the ground meat mixture. Remove from heat and spoon evenly into an 8 x 10 (20 x 25 cm) baking dish.

Spoon sweet potato mixture on top. Bake in the oven for 20 to 25 minutes.

Squash and Pumpkin Seed Salad

I eat salads every day, sometimes twice a day, so I love to find new combinations of ingredients. This salad contains so many healthy food groups and if you're trying to eat the rainbow – this is the ticket. Quinoa is a complete protein containing all nine essential amino acids that our body can't make on its own.

Serves 4

- ½ cup (90 g) package quinoa
- 3 cups (400 g) package prepared butternut squash, cut into 1 in (2.5 cm) cubes
- 1 small red onion, coarsely chopped
- 2 tablespoons (30 ml) olive oil, divided
- ¾ teaspoon (4 ml) salt, divided
- ¼ teaspoon (1 ml) pepper
- 3 tablespoons (45 ml) lemon juice, divided
- 2 cups (500 ml) broccoli florets, chopped
- 1 cup (250 ml) canned pinto or Romano beans, drained and rinsed
- ½ cup (125 ml) dried cherries
- ¼ cup (60 ml) roasted pumpkin seeds
- ½ cup (125 ml) crumbled goat feta

Cook quinoa following package directions.

Preheat the oven to 450°F (232°C).

Place the squash, onion, 1 tablespoon (15 ml) olive oil, ½ teaspoon (2.5 ml) of the salt and pepper on a baking sheet, stirring all ingredients to coat the squash with the oil. Bake in the oven until fork-tender, approximately 15-20 minutes. Drizzle with 1 tablespoon (15 ml) of the lemon juice.

Combine quinoa, squash mixture, broccoli, beans, cherries, pumpkin seeds, remaining 2 tablespoons (30 ml) lemon juice, remaining 1 tablespoon (15 ml) oil and remaining ¼ teaspoon (1.2 ml) salt in a large bowl. Top with feta before serving.

Carrot Cake

I made this cake for a birthday celebration and it was a huge hit. It is gluten and sugar free but you would never know it. It tastes like the real thing. I used walnuts but pecans are an option. It's a very fragile cake, so be extra careful taking it out of the baking pans. I used a cream cheese icing. If you are dairy free check out your local health food store for dairy free versions or skip the cream cheese icing and just eat the cake plain.

Serves 6

- 3/4 cup (175 ml) monk fruit sugar (or coconut sugar)
- 3/4 cup (175 ml) butter or coconut oil, softened
- 1 tablespoon (15 ml) black strap molasses (optional)
- 1 teaspoon (5 ml) pure vanilla extract
- 4 large eggs
- 2 1/2 cups (625 ml) almond flour
- 2 teaspoons (10 ml) baking powder
- 2 teaspoons (10 ml) cinnamon
- 1/2 teaspoon (5 ml) nutmeg
- 1/2 teaspoon (5 ml) sea salt
- 2 1/2 cup (625 ml) grated carrots, loosely packed
- 1 1/2 cups (375 ml) chopped walnuts, 1 cup (250 ml) for the batter, and 1/2 cup (125 ml) for the topping

---

Preheat the oven to 350°F (177°C). Line two 9 inch (22.5 cm) cake pans with parchment paper. Grease the bottom and sides.

In a large bowl, cream together the butter and monk fruit until fluffy. Beat in the molasses, and vanilla extract. Beat in the eggs, one at a time. Set aside.

In another bowl, mix together the almond flour, baking powder, cinnamon, and sea salt. Stir the dry ingredients into the wet ingredients.

Stir in the grated carrots. Fold in 1 cup (250 ml) of nuts, reserving the other 1/2 cup (125 ml) for the top of the cake.

Transfer the batter to the cake pans and bake for 30-35 minutes, until the top is springy to the touch or a toothpick comes out without any raw batter on it.

Let the cakes cool for about 10 minutes before transferring them to a plate or wire rack.

Roasted Carrot and Turmeric Soup

My husband loves carrot soup but I find it a bit too earthy for my taste. Roasting the carrots brings out their sweetness and results in a cleaner flavour. The addition of a few spices and tahini bumps up the nutrient content of this soup. Turmeric is anti-inflammatory, cancer preventing, and best of all it tastes good. The pumpkins seeds add a bit of crunchy fun!

Serves 4

- ¼ cup (60 ml) extra virgin olive oil
- 2 teaspoons (10 ml) ground turmeric
- 2 teaspoons (10 ml) ground cumin
- Sea salt and cracked black pepper
- 6 carrots, peeled and quartered lengthwise
- 1 onion, peeled and cut into wedges
- 68 oz./2 litres good-quality vegetable or chicken stock
- ¼ cup (60 ml) tahini, plus extra for garnish
- ¼ cup (3 g) coriander (cilantro) leaves
- Plain Greek-style (thick) yogurt, to serve
- 1 tablespoon (15 ml) pumpkins seeds, for garnish (optional)

Preheat the oven to 425°F (220°F).

Line 2 large baking trays with non-stick baking paper.

Place the oil, turmeric, cumin, salt and pepper in a large bowl and mix to combine. Add the carrot and onion and toss to combine. Divide between the 2 trays and roast for 25 minutes or until golden and just tender.

Transfer the roasted vegetables to a large saucepan. Add the stock and tahini and, using an immersion blender, blend until smooth. Place the soup over medium heat and bring to a simmer.

Divide between serving bowls and sprinkle with the coriander. Top with a swirl of yogurt and a swirl of extra tahini to serve.

Beet and Ginger Soup

This is an interesting combination of vegetables. The cauliflower gives it a richer texture compared to a standard beet soup, which is stock based. The ginger is healing and anti-inflammatory, and if you use a good quality bone broth, you're getting your daily collagen. This soup is good for the gut and the bones!

Serves 4

- 1 sweet onion, diced
- 2 celery stalks, diced
- 4 to 6 large beets, peeled and cut into chunks
- ½ head of cauliflower, cut into chunks
- 1-2 tablespoons (15 to 30 ml) of fresh ginger, grated
- 4 cups (1000 ml) bone or vegetable broth
- Salt and pepper to taste.

Place the ingredients into a large pot and bring to a boil. Turn the heat to low and simmer for 1 hour. Blend until smooth.

Serve.

Alternate method: Roast your vegetables with some olive oil and salt and pepper. Place in your blender with broth and purée. Place in a large pot, heat and serve.

Roasted Beet Salad with Horseradish Cream

I love roasted vegetables. Honestly, they're so easy and roasting brings out all the good flavours. Roasted beets are one of my favourites and they are excellent in this salad, which has everything: root vegetables, pomegranate (prebiotic), yogurt (probiotic), nuts, and healthy oils.

Serves 6

- 2 teaspoons (10 ml) extra-virgin olive oil
- 1 medium sweet onion, peeled and diced
- 1 celery stalk, diced
- 2 large garlic cloves, minced
- 2 lbs (1 kg) red beetroots, peeled and cut into 1-inch (2.5 cm) chunks
- 3 carrots, peeled and cut into ½ inch (1.25 cm) coins
- 1 teaspoon (5 ml) sea salt
- 1 bay leaf
- 2 fresh thyme sprigs
- ¼ cup (60 ml) pomegranate arils
- ¼ cup (60 ml) chopped nuts like pistachios or walnuts

Horseradish Cream with Dill

- ½ cup (125 ml) plain Greek yogurt
- 2 teaspoons (10 ml) horseradish, plus extra
- 2 teaspoons (10 ml) lemon juice
- ½ teaspoon (2.5 ml) maple syrup
- ¼ teaspoon (1 ml) sea salt
- 2 tablespoons (30 ml) fresh dill, minced, plus extra

In a large saucepan, heat oil over medium heat. Add onions, celery, and garlic, and stir to coat with oil. Sauté for 5 minutes, or until the onion is just beginning to soften. Stir in beets and carrots. Sprinkle with salt. Add bay leaf, thyme, and just enough water to cover vegetables. Bring to a gentle boil. Cover, reduce heat, and simmer for about 10 to 12 minutes, or just until vegetables are fork tender.

Meanwhile, make cream. In a small bowl, mix all ingredients. Set aside.

Drain vegetables and transfer to a large, shallow bowl. Remove bay leaf and thyme stems. Cool until no longer hot, about 15 minutes. Scatter with pomegranate and nuts. Drizzle with horseradish cream and scatter fresh dill over top. Serve at once.

Roasted Carrots with Beet Purée, Goat Cheese, and Hazelnuts

This recipe combines roasted carrots with goat cheese and hazelnuts. Goat cheese is healthier for you than cow cheese because it actually helps restore the gut microbiome. This dish may seem like a lot of effort but it's worth it.

Serves 6

- 1½ lbs (680 kg) small, multi-coloured carrots with tops
- 2 tablespoons (30 ml) extra-virgin olive oil
- ½ teaspoon (2.5 ml) kosher salt, plus more to taste
- ¼ teaspoon (1 ml) black pepper, plus more to taste
- ½ cup (125 ml) cold unsalted butter, diced
- ½ cup (125 ml) hazelnuts, toasted and crushed
- 3 tablespoons (45 ml) sherry vinegar
- 1 tablespoon (15 ml) fresh lemon juice
- Red beet purée (recipe follows)
- Young dandelion greens or arugula
- 4 oz. (113 g) goat cheese or other young aged goat cheese

For the carrots:

Preheat the oven to 450°F (232°C).

Remove the tops from carrots, reserving ¼ cup (60 ml). Discard remaining tops or reserve for another use. Cut any large carrots in half so they are all roughly the same size. Toss together carrots, olive oil, salt and pepper in a large bowl. Spread in an even layer on a rimmed baking sheet.

Roast in a preheated oven until carrots are browned in spots and tender, about 20 minutes, stirring once halfway through cooking.

While carrots roast, melt butter in a medium saucepan over medium. Cook, stirring often, until butter browns and smells nutty, about 5 minutes. Remove from heat and let cool for 1 minute. Carefully stir in hazelnuts, sherry vinegar, lemon juice, and salt and pepper to taste.

For the beet purée:

- 1 lb (454 g) medium-size red beets, trimmed
- 1 tablespoon (15 ml) extra-virgin olive oil
- 1 ¼ teaspoon (6 ml) sea salt, divided
- ½ cup (125 ml) avocado oil
- 2 tablespoons (30 ml) finely chopped shallot
- 2 tablespoons (30 ml) water
- 1 ½ teaspoon (7.5 ml) fresh cilantro leaves
- 1 ½ teaspoon (7.5 ml) red wine vinegar
- Pinch of black pepper

Preheat the oven to 400°F (204°C).

Toss beets with olive oil and ½ teaspoon (2.5 ml) salt. Place beets in a roasting pan; add a splash of water. Cover tightly with aluminum foil, and roast in a preheated oven until tender when pierced, about 1 hour and 30 minutes. Remove foil, and let cool for 15 minutes. Peel beets then roughly chop.

Place avocado oil, shallots, 2 tablespoons (30 ml) water, cilantro, vinegar, and remaining ¾ teaspoon (4 ml) salt in a blender, and process until blended, about 5 seconds. Add beets, and process until smooth, about 40 seconds, stopping to scrape down sides as needed. Stir in black pepper.

Spread red beet purée in the centre of a large platter; arrange carrots on top. Spoon hazelnut sauce over carrots. Tuck dandelion greens and reserved carrot tops around carrots. Using a vegetable peeler, shave cheese over carrots.

Susanne's Tip: Clean up as you cook for a more pleasant experience overall.

Make Ahead Anytime Dill and Beet Salad

Best served chilled, this isn't a last-minute recipe but it's a great make ahead dish for a party or luncheon. It's simple and once prepared can sit in the fridge for days and still taste great when served. Dill is part of the celery family and has many of the same health benefits. It's packed with flavonoids and studies have found that it can prevent Type 2 diabetes, heart attack, and stroke.

Serves 4

- 2 tablespoons (30 ml) mayonnaise
- 2 tablespoons (30 ml) apple cider vinegar
- 1 tablespoon (15 ml) olive oil
- 1 teaspoon (5 ml) sea salt
- **Freshly ground black pepper**
- **8 medium beets**
- **1 ½ cups (375 ml) loosely packed dill fronds**

In a lidded jar, combine the mayonnaise, vinegar, olive oil, and salt, and season with pepper. Seal the jar tightly, shake vigorously until incorporated, and then chill for up to 1 week.

Scrub the beets and slice off the tips and stems. (Leave the skins on to help the beets retain their colour and nutrients when you boil them.) Place the beets in a large pot and add enough cold water to cover. Simmer, covered, and cook until a fork easily pierces the centre of the thickest beet, 20 to 30 minutes. Drain the beets and rinse with cold water. Once cool, peel the skin from the beets with your hands. (It should slide off fairly easily.) Halve the beets, then cut into very thin slices, about ⅛ inch thick, and store in an airtight container or Ziploc bag, chilled up to 3 days.

Mince the dill. Transfer the beets to a serving bowl. Pour the dressing over the beets, add the dill, and toss together until everything is evenly coated.

Serve cold. Store leftovers in an airtight container, chilled for up to 1 week.

The Rest of the Rainbow

There are many other vegetables to explore. To maintain adequate nutritional intake, we should be eating at least 10 vegetable servings a day. It's wise to eat the rainbow. This means eating vegetables and fruits of different colours to get all the essential micronutrients. Red foods contain antioxidants like lycopene and anthocyanins and orange foods contain carotenoids, which convert to vitamin A in the body. Green foods contain chlorophyll and sulforaphane.

Fill your plate ¾ full of vegetables and ¼ other. Variety is the key to keeping your diet exciting. Eating the same things all the time leads to boredom and food sensitivities –and when we're bored, we all tend to reach for unhealthy options to fill our bellies.

Asparagus Chopped Salad with Tomatoes

Asparagus is one of my favourite green vegetables. I eat it several times a week. It has amino acids that protect our liver cells and has even been recommended as a cure for a hangover. It prevents UTIs, stimulates the libido, and improves mood. This recipe also has peas and tomatoes, so it's very colourful and festive.

Serves 4

- 12 oz. (375 g) asparagus, trimmed
- 1 cup (250 ml) peas
- 3 tablespoons (45 ml) red wine vinegar
- 1 teaspoon (5 ml) Dijon mustard
- ½ teaspoon (2.5 ml) salt
- ¼ teaspoon (1 ml) pepper
- 2 large tomatoes, chopped
- 1 sweet pepper, chopped
- 1 tablespoon (15 ml) red onion, chopped

Cut asparagus on the diagonal into small pieces. Cook peas in boiling water for 2 minutes. Add asparagus and boil until vegetables are just tender-crisp, about 3 minutes. Drain and rinse under cold water until chilled. Drain well and pat dry.

In a large bowl, whisk together the vinegar, mustard, salt and pepper; gradually whisk in oil until blended. Add cooked vegetables, tomatoes, red onion and sweet pepper; toss to coat.

Did you know that steaming your veggies helps preserve their nutritional benefits? You can steam using a double boiler or a metal steamer.

Roasted Tomatoes

This dish is great served as a quick appetizer with some gluten free bread or crackers. Cooked tomatoes have a much deeper taste than raw ones, and the spices and balsamic excite the palate. It's easy and fast and a great way to use up your tomatoes.

Serves 8 to 10 as appetizer

- 15 to 18 Roma tomatoes
- ¾ cup (175 ml) olive oil
- 1 tablespoon (15 ml) balsamic vinegar
- 1 teaspoon (5 ml) Italian seasoning
- 1 teaspoon (5 ml) sea salt
- ¼ teaspoon (1 ml) freshly ground black pepper
- 3 cloves garlic, minced
- ½ cup (125 ml) flat leafed parsley, finely chopped
- 4 ½ ounces (128 g) of soft goat cheese.

Preheat the oven to 350°F (177°C).

Quarter the tomatoes and discard the juicy pulp from the inside. Place the tomatoes in a glass or ceramic 9 x 13 (33 x 23 cm) baking dish along with the oil, balsamic, Italian seasoning, salt and pepper.

Roast the tomatoes for 1 hour and 15 minutes, stirring every once in a while. Remove from the oven and immediately stir in the garlic and parsley and allow the tomatoes to cool slightly. Scatter the goat cheese over the top.

Serve warm or room temperature.

Sweet Pea and Asparagus Soup

I love different combinations of vegetables thrown together to make great tasting soups and this is one of my faves. Asparagus helps with wound healing because it stimulates collagen production. Just one more reason to make this soup!

Serves 8 to 10

- 2 tablespoons (30 ml) unsalted butter
- 3 cloves garlic, minced
- 2 medium shallots, finely diced
- 1 large bundle asparagus, ends trimmed and stalks cut into 1-inch (2.5 cm) pieces
- Sea salt
- Black pepper
- 3 cups (750 ml) green peas, fresh or frozen (thawed)
- 3 - 4 cups (750 to 1000 ml) broth, chicken, turkey, or vegetable
- ½ cup (125 ml) parsley, finely chopped, plus some for garnish
- 3 - 4 tablespoons (45 to 60 ml) mint, finely chopped, plus some for garnish
- 2 teaspoons (10 ml) grated lemon zest
- ½ cup (125 ml) unsweetened coconut, or nut milk or dairy milk or cream
- 2 teaspoons (10 ml) lemon juice (optional)
- Sour cream (optional)

For the soup, place a large pot over medium heat. Melt the butter and cook the garlic and shallots until just softened, approximately 2 to 3 minutes. Add in the asparagus and season with salt and pepper. Cook for 3 minutes before adding the peas, then 3 cups (750 ml) of the broth. Bring to a boil. Turn heat down to low; simmer until vegetables are just tender, about 3 to 4 minutes.

Add the parsley, mint, zest, and milk. Pour into a blender or use a hand mixer and blend on high.

Season with salt and pepper and a squirt of lemon juice. If the soup is too thick, add the additional cup of broth.

Serve hot or cold. Add a dollop of sour cream before serving (optional).

Asparagus with Lemon-Basil-Yogurt Sauce

Asparagus is delicious on its own but with a lovely sauce it's a little bit of heaven. Just make sure you don't over cook the asparagus – it's meant to be firm. Asparagus is a prebiotic and when we pair it with yogurt, which is a probiotic, we create a dish that will help heal the gut. Three to four servings of fermented foods a day reduce our inflammatory markers as well.

Serves 4

- 1-pound (454 g) asparagus tips
- ½ cup (125 ml) grass-fed Greek yogurt
- 3 tablespoons (45 ml) fresh basil, chopped
- 1 teaspoon (5 ml) lemon zest
- 2 tablespoons (30 ml) fresh lemon juice
- 1 tablespoon (15 ml) honey, maple syrup or other sweetener
- ¼ teaspoon (1 ml) salt
- ¼ teaspoon (1 ml) black pepper
- 2 cups of ice

Bring a pot of water to boil, add asparagus, and cook for 2 minutes or until tender, then drain. Immediately put the asparagus into ice water, then drain again. This stops the asparagus from cooking further.

Combine yogurt, basil, lemon rind and juice, sweetener, salt and pepper. Pour over the asparagus.

Pizza with a Spaghetti Squash Crust

To be honest, this is not a real pizza...but it's a great alternative if you're not eating grains. I love spaghetti squash with tomato sauce and parmesan cheese but this is an upgrade, and by adding lots of vegetables you get your 10 to 12 servings for the day. Have fun with it by using different toppings and sauces.

4 to 6 servings

- 1 large spaghetti squash
- 1 tablespoon (15 ml) olive oil
- 2 large eggs
- ¼ cup (60 ml) coconut flour
- ½ teaspoon (2.5 ml) sea salt
- ¼ teaspoon (1 ml) black pepper
- 1 (15 oz./425 g) can pizza sauce
- ½ cup (125 ml) basil pesto
- 1 cup (125 g) red pepper, chopped
- 1 cup (125 g) green pepper, chopped
- 1 cup (100 g) red onion, diced
- ½ cup (40 g) mushrooms, sliced
- 1 teaspoon (5 ml) garlic, minced
- Dried oregano and basil to taste
- 4 oz. (113 g) fresh cheese, thinly sliced, optional

Preheat the oven to 400°F (204°C).

Cut the spaghetti squash in half lengthwise and remove the seeds. Drizzle the insides with olive oil and place face down on a baking sheet. Bake for 35 to 40 minutes, or until knife slides easily into the back of the squash.

Remove the squash from the oven and allow it to cool. With a fork, break up the flesh of the squash into strings of spaghetti. Remove excess moisture from the squash by pressing the strings between two layers of paper towels.

In a large bowl, combine the squash, eggs, coconut flour, salt and pepper to form the crust mixture.

Prepare a baking sheet with parchment paper and place the mixture on the tray. Form into a large crust about ⅛ inch (0.3 cm) thick. Bake for 20 to 25 minutes. Remove from oven and spread the pizza sauce evenly over the crust, followed by the basil pesto, vegetables, garlic, seasonings, and cheese (optional). Return to the oven for 10 to 15 minutes, or until the vegetables are slightly tender and cheese has melted.

Overnight Yogurt and Oatmeal - Page 126

Have Fun with Fermented Foods

Fermented foods such as yogurt, kefir, miso, kimchi, kombucha, tempeh, fermented vegetables, sourdough, sauerkraut, and cheese contain healthy microbes and probiotics. These living bacteria become metabolically active in the gut and aid in absorption of nutrients.

Fermented foods have been shown to alter brain activity. When consumed along with prebiotic foods (high fiber foods) they help grow good bacteria and enzymes needed for digestion. They also play a role in healing the gut lining, making the immune system more robust. As the connection between the gut and serotonin has been discussed, and the link between a healthy gut and a healthy mind has been proven, it's only smart to include more fermented foods into our meals.

Overnight Yogurt and Oatmeal

I often get asked, "What can I eat for breakfast that's fast and healthy?" Overnight oatmeal fits the bill as long as you prepare it the day before. I usually make a large enough recipe to have a few times during the week. This version includes yogurt instead of milk. Buy full fat, grass-fed yogurt whenever possible. If you're dairy-free, try coconut, almond, or cashew yogurt instead.

Serves 4

- **1 to 2 tablespoons (15 to 30 ml) of butter**
- **2 oz. (50 g) sprouted gluten free oats**
- **1 tablespoon (15 ml) sunflower seeds**
- **1 tablespoon (15 ml) pumpkin seeds**
- **5 to 10 nuts, chopped**
- **1 to 2 tablespoons (15 to 30 ml) honey, or to taste**
- **2 oz. (50 g) blueberries**
- **3 oz. (75 g) raspberries**
- **7 oz. (200 g) grass-fed yogurt**

Prepare jars and lids.

Melt the butter in a small frying pan over medium-high heat. Add the oats and seeds. Stir fry for 2 to 3 minutes or until the oats and seeds start to toast. Add the nuts and remove from heat. Add honey.

Set aside and let cool.

Divide the fruit between jars and press down slightly. Spoon the yogurt on top and place cooled oat mixture on top of it. Cover with lid and chill until needed.

Yogurt with Feta Dip

This is such an easy dip. If you're not a mint fan, try dill instead. Serve with crudités or use as a dressing or topping for lettuce or roasted vegetables.

Makes 1 ½ cups (300 ml)

- 1 cup (250 ml) plain grass-fed Greek yogurt
- ½ cup (75 g) feta cheese
- 1 lemon, zested and juiced
- 1 cup (250 ml) fresh oregano leaves, stems removed
- 1 cup (250 ml) fresh green onions
- 1 cup (250 ml) fresh parsley leaves, hard stems removed
- 1 cup (250 ml) fresh mint leaves, stems removed
- 1 garlic clove, roughly chopped
- ¼ cup (60 ml) olive oil
- Salt and pepper to taste

Add the yogurt, feta, lemon zest and juice, oregano, green onions, parsley, mint, garlic, and oil to a blender or food processor and blend until combined and smooth. Adjust the seasoning with salt and pepper and serve in a bowl.

Garnish with an extra drizzle of olive oil.

Pan-Seared Tofu

Tofu is made of condensed soy milk. In the processing, a coagulant is used to help solidify the bean curd and form it into a block similar to how cheese is made. It's high in protein and amino acid and rich in vitamins and minerals such as zinc, iron, and selenium. Its low-calorie count makes it a nutrient dense food.

Because soybeans also contain isoflavones that activate estrogen receptors in the body, they're revered by vegans and health nuts alike. It's the isoflavones that may offer protection from heart disease, diabetes, cancer, bone health and, of course, brain disorders.

It also contains what are called anti-nutrients. These are nutrients that are not good for our health, like trypsin inhibitors and phytates. Soaking, cooking, sprouting, or fermenting all reduce, but don't totally eliminate, the anti-nutrients. Eat only fermented soy and avoid all processed types.

This recipe is super easy and can be served as a side dish or your main protein with a soup or salad.

Serves 2 to 4

- 1 (14 oz./397 g) package extra firm tofu
- 1 cup (250 ml) gluten-free flour blend
- 2 tablespoons (30 ml) avocado or coconut oil

Cut the tofu into 1 inch (2.5 cm) thick slabs. Place two layers of paper towels on a cutting board, place tofu slices on top and then cover with two more layers of paper towels. Place a heavy baking dish on top of the tofu and weigh it down with cans of food or anything heavy. This procedure will force the moisture out of the tofu. This will take at least 30 minutes.

Remove the tofu from the paper towels and dredge it in flour. Shake off the excess.

Heat the oil in a large skillet over medium heat. Add tofu one piece of time. It should be sizzling. Fill the pan with the slices in one layer without them touching. Cook until the underside is golden brown, 5 to 6 minutes. Flip over with spatula and cook the other side until golden brown, 5 to 6 minutes. Repeat with remaining slices.

Susanne's Tip: Tofu comes in varying degrees of softness, from silky smooth to very firm. Experiment with the texture that you like best.

I See, You See, We All See Fish and Seafood

In order to keep your brain healthy, you need to regularly consume DHA, an omega-3 fatty acid that goes straight to your brain. It's recommended to eat two four-ounce servings of fish per week. Oily fish have the most DHA. What your brain doesn't need is high levels of mercury and plastics, so it's important to choose your fish carefully and make sure it is caught ethically.

Slow-Baked Salmon

I discovered only recently that cooking fish slowly enhances the flavours and results in moist and delicious fish. The spices add to the flavour profile and the mayonnaise helps keep the fish moist. A great dish to serve to guests or on a buffet table.

8 Servings

- 1 3 lb (1.36 kg) organic or wild-caught salmon filet
- 4 tablespoons (60 ml) extra virgin olive oil, divided
- 2 tablespoons (30 ml) smooth Dijon mustard
- 2 teaspoons (10 ml) sea salt
- ½ to 1 teaspoon (2.5 to 5 ml) dried chili flakes
- 1 lemon, zested and halved
- ½ cup (125 ml) avocado mayonnaise
- ¼ cup (60 ml) fresh tarragon leaves, finely chopped
- ¼ cup (60 ml) fresh chives, finely chopped
- Sea salt
- Freshly ground black pepper
- Lemon wedges, for serving

Preheat the oven to 300°F (149°C).

Dry off the salmon with a paper towel. Coat the bottom of a baking sheet with 2 tablespoons (30 ml) of the oil and place the salmon skin-side down on the sheet. Rub the flesh side of the salmon with the remaining oil and brush the Dijon over the top. Sprinkle with the salt and chili flakes and squeeze half the lemon over the top.

Bake the salmon approximately 28 to 35 minutes or until springy to the touch or until center flakes when tested with a fork.

Meanwhile, squeeze the juice from the remaining lemon half into a small bowl. Add in the zest, mayonnaise, tarragon, and chives. Stir until blended. Stir in salt and pepper.

Remove the salmon from the oven and place it on a platter with the tarragon-chive mayonnaise on the side. Garnish with lemon wedges. Serve with a spatula, leaving the skin behind.

Serve cold or right out of the oven.

Did you know that rinsing feta cheese before use eliminates much of the salt?

Dill, Shrimp and Feta Cheese Salad

Our family has made a conscious decision to avoid seafood from the ocean for environmental, humanitarian, and health reasons. If you eat seafood, do your research before you purchase. There are sustainable options; they may cost more but I feel it's worth it. This salad has all my favourites: veggies, dill, feta, and the cleanest shrimp you can find. The dressing makes the salad!

Serves 4

- 1-pound (454 g) shrimp, shelled and deveined
- 3 green onions, including tops, sliced thin
- ½ medium size cucumber, peeled, seeded, and chopped
- ½ cup (125 ml) diced red pepper
- ¼ teaspoon (1 ml) black pepper
- ¼ cup (125 ml) feta cheese, rinsed and crumbled

Dressing:

- 2 tablespoons (30 ml) lemon juice
- 2 tablespoons (30 ml) olive oil
- 1 tablespoon (15 ml) white wine vinegar
- 1 teaspoon (5 ml) Dijon mustard
- 1 clove garlic
- 2 tablespoons (30 ml) fresh dill, snipped, or dried dill to taste

---

In a heavy saucepan over medium-high heat, bring a quart of water to a boil. Add shrimp and cook until just firm, about 2 minutes. Drain and rinse under cold water to stop the cooking, and drain again.

Place the shrimp in a large bowl and add the green onions, cucumber, red pepper, dill, and cheese.

In a small bowl, whisk together the lemon juice, olive oil, vinegar, mustard, garlic, and black pepper. Pour over the shrimp mixture and toss gently to mix.

Did you know that rinsing feta cheese before use eliminates much of the salt?

Herbed Salmon Burgers with Cucumber-Radish Slaw and Gribiche

This recipe is a little more labour intensive than just throwing the salmon in the oven, but it's impressive to serve and delicious to eat. Gribiche is a cold egg sauce used in French cuisine and takes this burger from good to outstanding, as does the cucumber radish slaw. It all goes together so well that this will become a regular in your dinner repertoire.

Serves 4

Patties:

- 1 ½ lbs (750 g) organic salmon fillet, skin removed
- 1 large egg, lightly beaten
- ¼ cup (60 ml) gluten free panko bread crumbs
- ¼ cup (60 ml) chives, finely chopped
- ¼ cup (60 ml) mixed herbs (parsley, tarragon and/or dill), finely chopped
- ½ teaspoon (2.5 ml) salt
- ¼ teaspoon (1 ml) freshly ground pepper
- Olive oil for forming the patties
- 4 gluten free buns

Gribiche:

- 1 large hard-boiled egg, peeled
- 1 tablespoon (15 ml) Dijon mustard
- 1 tablespoon (15 ml) white wine vinegar
- 3 tablespoons (45 ml) extra virgin olive oil
- 1 tablespoon (15 ml) small capers, rinsed, patted dry
- 2 cornichons, finely chopped
- 1 tablespoon (15 ml) tarragon, finely chopped
- 1 tablespoon (15 ml) chives, finely chopped
- Salt and pepper to taste

Cucumber-Radish Slaw:

- 1 tablespoon (15 ml) granulated sugar substitute such as monk fruit or honey
- 2 tablespoons (30 ml) white wine vinegar
- 1 piece English cucumber, 4 inches (10 cm) long
- 2 radishes
- Salt to taste
- 1 teaspoon (5 ml) extra virgin olive oil

For the patties: Cut salmon into 1-inch (2.5 cm) chunks. Place in a food processor. Pulse until coarsely chopped and clumping together – it will take seconds. (Don't over-mix or the cooked patty will be rubbery.) In a mixing bowl, combine salmon, egg, panko, chives, herbs, salt and pepper. Mix thoroughly. Using well-oiled hands, divide into 4 even balls. Form balls into patties to fit buns. Cover and refrigerate at least 3 hours and up to 1 day.

For the gribiche: Separate egg yolk and white. Finely chop white and set aside. Place egg yolk in a small mixing bowl with mustard and vinegar. Mash yolk with a fork then whisk until smooth. Slowly drizzle oil while whisking to form emulsified dressing. Fold in capers, cornichons, herbs, and egg white. Season with salt and pepper. Cover and refrigerate up to 1 day.

For the cucumber-radish slaw: Whisk sugar substitute and vinegar in a mixing bowl until sugar is dissolved. Thinly slice cucumber and radishes on mandolin or with a sharp knife. Add to bowl and season generously with salt. Mix thoroughly. Cover and refrigerate 1 hour. Drain mixture and stir in olive oil. Cover and refrigerate up to 4 hours.

*Preheat the grill to medium-high. Grill patties until just cooked through, 3 to 4 minutes per side. Smear bun bottoms with gribiche. Top with patties. Top patties with some cucumber-radish slaw. Cover with bun tops. Serve immediately.

*If you do not have a grill, try them in the air fryer or bake them in the oven.

Make Mighty Organic Meats a Priority

The discussion surrounding why we should eat organic meat versus conventionally raised meats could fill up this whole book, so I'll be brief. There are environmental issues, health consequences, and ethical considerations involved in buying and consuming meats. We've been told that meat is bad for us and that saturated fats will kill us, but much has been written to debunk these myths. We now understand that fats are not the problem – sugar and refined carbs are the culprit.

I encourage you to do some research and learn more about how your food gets to your plate and what you're consuming. Whatever the animal eats is also what you are eating. If the cow is fed corn, you are eating corn in your steak. If the animal has been exposed to hormones or antibiotics, so will you be. Livestock that is fed grass and alfalfa have higher levels of omega-3 fatty acids than conventionally raised meat.

Susanne's Tip: Slice all meat across the grain for optimal tenderness.

Beef and Broccoli

Traditional Chinese takeout is loaded with MSG, vegetable oils, soy, corn, and gluten, and therefore, not a healthy option for takeout. Try making this recipe as an alternative. Flank steak is economical and this dish will satisfy your craving for Chinese food. Try the sesame seeds as a garnish, but also to give it some added texture and nutrients.

Serves 4 to 6

- 2 pounds (.907 kg) flank steak
- ⅔ cups (158 ml) coconut amino or gluten free soy sauce
- 2 tablespoons (30 ml) arrowroot powder
- 3 ½ teaspoon (17.5 ml) toasted sesame oil
- 1 ¼ teaspoon (6 ml) apple cider vinegar
- 4 tablespoons (60 ml) avocado oil or ghee
- 4 cloves garlic, minced
- 1 teaspoon (5 ml) fresh ginger, peeled and minced
- 5 cups (355 g) broccoli florets
- ⅓ cup (80 ml) beef bone broth
- Fine sea salt
- ¼ teaspoon (1 ml) ground white pepper
- Your favourite rice or quinoa
- Sesame seeds (for garnish, optional)

Place the steak in the freezer for 20 minutes to make it easier to slice. Cut it on the diagonal into ⅛ inch (3 mm) slices, then cut each slice into 2 inch (5 cm) pieces. Place the steak pieces in a shallow bowl. In a separate bowl, whisk together the coconut amino, arrowroot, 3 teaspoons (15 ml) of the sesame oil, and the vinegar and pour the mixture over the steak, stirring to coat each piece well. Marinate for 30 minutes.

Heat 2 tablespoons (30 ml) of the oil in a wok or large skillet over medium-high heat. Stir in the garlic and ginger, and let them sizzle in the hot oil for about 30 seconds. Stir in the broccoli, tossing the florets in the hot oil until they turn bright green and almost tender, 5 to 7 minutes. Remove the broccoli from the wok and set aside.

Add the remaining 2 tablespoons (30 ml) of oil to the wok. Let the pan get very hot again. With tongs, add the marinated meat to the wok in a single layer, reserving the marinating liquid and working in batches to avoid crowding the meat. Do not stir the meat until it has browned, about 1 minute. Flip the meat and cook the other side for 30 seconds more, then transfer the meat to a clean plate to rest.

Pour the reserved marinade into the wok along with the bone broth, ½ teaspoon (2.5 ml) salt, and white pepper. Cook over medium-high heat until the sauce starts to thicken, about 45 seconds. Add the beef and broccoli back to the wok and toss to coat. Season with salt to taste and finish with the remaining ½ teaspoon (2.5 ml) sesame oil. Serve warm over your favourite rice or grain.

Did you know that the amount of fat used determines the method? A little fat is sautéing, a generous amount is pan-frying, and immersing the food in fat is deep frying.

Turkey Meatballs

Turkey is high in tryptophan, an amino acid that is good for the brain. Tryptophan regulates serotonin levels and serotonin helps regulate mood and sleep. Add some veggies in the form of zucchini, some spices, and you have a tasty, low calorie, high protein meal that's loaded with vitamins and minerals. The pairing options are endless. Make a batch ahead and freeze them for a rainy day.

Serves 8

- 2 pounds (.907 kg) ground turkey
- 1 cup (250 ml) shredded zucchini with the liquid squeezed out (measured before squeezing)
- 2 large eggs
- 4 large garlic cloves, grated
- 2 tablespoons (30 ml) onion flakes or powder
- 1 teaspoon (5 ml) dried oregano
- 1 teaspoon (5 ml) sea salt
- Ground pepper to taste

Preheat the oven to 375°F (190°C) and line 2 large baking sheets with unbleached parchment paper and grease with avocado oil or use a silicone baking mat.

In a large bowl, add ground turkey, zucchini, eggs, garlic, onion powder, oregano, salt and pepper. Mix well with your hands. Using a scoop or your hands, make approximately 45 meatballs and lay on a baking sheet.

Bake for 15 minutes, turn and toss with spatula and bake for 5 more minutes.

Serve hot or freeze.

Susanne's Tip: Once meatballs are completely cooled on the baking sheet, place the baking sheet in the freezer until the meatballs are frozen. Remove the sheet and place the meat balls in a container separated by waxed paper to prevent them from clumping.

Orange Chicken with Brussels Sprouts

I love the combination of fruit and chicken: oranges, lemons, or raspberries are my favourites. This recipe pairs oranges and chicken thighs. The addition of Brussels sprouts and cranberry provides great texture and taste. You only need this dish to feel satisfied and get a pile of nutrients.

Serves 4

For the chicken:

- 4 boneless, skin-on pasture-raised chicken thighs
- ½ teaspoon (2.5 ml) dried sage
- ½ teaspoon (2.5 ml) dried rosemary
- ½ teaspoon (2.5 ml) dried thyme
- ½ teaspoon (2.5 ml) dried oregano
- ½ teaspoon (2.5 ml) paprika
- ¼ teaspoon (1 ml) Himalayan pink salt or sea salt
- ¼ teaspoon (1 ml) ground pepper
- 2 to 3 tablespoon (30 to 45 ml) fresh orange juice
- A few orange wedges
- 1 tablespoon (15 ml) avocado oil

For the Brusselss Sprouts:

- 1-pound (454 g) Brusselss sprouts
- Salt and pepper
- Avocado oil

For the Cranberry Sauce:

- 5 oz. (140 g) fresh cranberries
- 1 tablespoon (15 ml) monk fruit sweetener or Swerve, or more to taste
- Zest of 1 orange
- 2 tablespoons (30 ml) fresh orange juice
- ¼ cup (60 ml) water, or more as needed
- ½ teaspoon (2.5 ml) cinnamon

Preheat the oven to 375°F (190°C).

To prepare the chicken: Pat the chicken dry with paper towels. Combine the spices in a small bowl and season the chicken generously with the mixture. Place the chicken in a shallow bowl and add the orange juice, orange wedges, and avocado oil. Cover and marinate in the fridge for 30 minutes.

To prepare the Brusselss sprouts: Cut the sprouts in half, place in a bowl, drizzle with oil, and season with salt and pepper. Toss to coat. Place the chicken on one half of a large sheet pan and the sprouts on the other. Bake for 20 minutes. Turn the oven to low broil and broil both the chicken and the sprouts for 5 more minutes.

To make the cranberry sauce: While the chicken and Brussels sprouts are cooking, add the cranberry sauce ingredients to a large saucepan and cook over medium-low heat for 15 to 20 minutes, until the cranberries pop and a sauce forms. If it's too thick, you can add more water or orange juice. You can taste and see if you want to add more sweetener, but keep in mind that the tartness of the sauce will balance out the sweetness of the chicken and Brussels sprouts. Add cinnamon to enhance the flavour.

To serve, spread some cranberry sauce on a plate. Add the chicken and Brussels sprouts on top.

Beans, Beans, the Magical Fruit

These disease fighting legumes are full of protein, fiber, and nutrients. In fact, they're a vegetable and a protein. They have 15 grams of plant protein per cup. A true superfood, they're inexpensive and versatile. Beans are full of copper, folate, iron, magnesium, potassium, and zinc. They help to control blood sugar in Type 2 diabetics. Beans contain resistant starch, a type of fiber that increases your good gut bacteria and may control inflammation and helps you feel full. Eat a variety of beans as they all have different nutrients, and don't forget to soak them overnight to remove the lectins. You can also use canned beans, just remember to drain and rinse off the salt.

Bean Varieties:

Black beans are full of phytonutrients including magnesium and quercetin. These beans aid digestion, keep your heart working and strengthen your bones. They're good with rice and a staple in Tex-Mex recipes.

Cannellini beans are an excellent source of fiber, folate, iron, and magnesium. They may help lower your blood sugar and are a good source of protein. They have thin skins so if you over cook, they will get mushy. Good in salads and as a thickener in soups. Favoured in Italian cooking.

Chickpeas are also called garbanzo beans. Their creamy texture makes them great for dips and sandwiches. They're rich in choline, an important nutrient for maintaining brain function. The magnesium found in chickpeas is a key mineral in nerve function.

Great Northern beans are grainy with tougher skins, so nice for soups. A good substitute for cannellini beans, they are rich in nutrients like zinc, selenium, and thiamin. High in fiber and protein, they are another bean that helps control blood sugar.

Lentils are like a sponge for spices and flavouring and star in a variety of cuisines. They're rich in pantothenic acid, which makes the chemical coenzyme A, a critical ingredient for brain function. Use canned if you're avoiding gluten because dried beans are often contaminated with glutinous grains.

Pinto beans have a hearty flavour and texture. Commonly eaten whole or mashed and fried. Low in calories and high in fiber, they may help reduce cholesterol and blood sugar levels. They are excellent for healing the gut.

Red kidney beans are famous for being a main ingredient in chili. Consumption aids in weight management and prevention of metabolic syndrome, a condition that leads to many diseases. One word of caution: it is a very common food allergy or sensitivity.

Susanne's Tip: Increase your bean intake gradually to avoid flatulence and drink plenty of water to help move the fiber through your system faster.

Cooking Dried Legumes and Beans

1. Pick through your beans, legumes, and lentils to discard shrivelled or discoloured ones before soaking.
2. Rinse under water and drain well.
3. Soak beans and legumes in water (1:3 ratio) and put in the refrigerator. You do not need to soak lentils, split peas, or black-eyed peas.
4. The quick soak method involves placing beans in a pot with a 1:3 ratio of water and bringing to a boil. Turn off heat, place a lid on the pot and let soak at room temperature for 3 to 4 hours.
5. Rinse beans thoroughly after soaking.
6. Cook beans in fresh water in a 1:3 ratio of beans to water. Never use the soaking water to cook the beans.
7. To cook, simmer uncovered, stirring often for approximately 45 minutes. Cook until tender, adding more hot water if needed.
8. Drain and enjoy.

Beans on Toast

We eat baked beans for breakfast, so why not other types of beans? Beans on toast is the new avocado on toast and the options are endless. Below is just one option. It uses butter beans seasoned with tomatoes, onion, and parsley for a flavour explosion.

Serves 2

- 1 teaspoon (5 ml) coconut oil
- 1 small onion, peeled, halved and thinly sliced
- ½ teaspoon (2.5 ml) smoked paprika
- 14 oz. (400 g) can of diced tomatoes
- 14 oz. (400 g) can of butter beans, drained
- 2 thick slices of gluten-free bread
- Couple sprigs of parsley, leaves chopped
- Sea salt and pepper to taste

Heat the coconut oil in a medium saucepan over medium-low heat until melted. Add the onion, paprika, salt and pepper. Stir to coat, then cover and cook for 5 to 7 minutes until onion has softened, stirring occasionally.

Add chopped tomatoes and butter beans, bring to a boil, then reduce the heat to low and simmer for 15 minutes until cooked through, stirring occasionally.

Toast the bread, serve the beans on top, and sprinkle with parsley.

Black Bean Dip

Black beans are the superfood of beans. They're high in fiber and protein and loaded with nutrients. This recipe is easy to throw together for an impromptu get together or outdoor barbeque.

Serves 6

- 1 garlic clove
- 1-15 oz. (425 g) can black beans, rinsed and drained
- ¼ cup (60 ml) onions, chopped
- ¼ cup (60 ml) salsa
- 2 tablespoons (30 ml) lime juice, or to taste
- ¼ cup (60 ml) fresh cilantro, plus 2 tablespoons (30 ml) chopped
- Additional fresh cilantro for garnish
- ¼ teaspoon (1 ml) chipotle chili powder
- 1 teaspoon (5 ml) ground cumin
- ½ teaspoon (2.5 ml) sea salt
- 1 to 2 tablespoons (15 to 30 ml) water (optional)
- 1 small tomato, seeded and finely diced

Place garlic, black beans, onions, salsa, lime juice, chili powder, cumin, and salt in a blender or a food processor. Blend to a dip-like consistency. If the mixture is too thick, add water by the tablespoon. Taste and adjust seasonings, adding more salt or lime juice as needed.

Transfer to a bowl, cover, and refrigerate to chill for a minimum of 15 minutes. Garnish with tomatoes and chopped cilantro; serve with vegetables and chips. Can be stored for 3 days in an airtight container.

Baked Cannellini Bean and Sun-Dried Tomato Dip

I like cannellini beans for their mild taste and versatility. You can mix them with a lot of foods and they won't overpower the other ingredients. In this recipe, we have sun-dried tomatoes, one of my favourite additions. I use them when I want to add flavour to a mild or bland recipe. Serve this dip with raw veggies to increase your nutritional profile for the day!

Makes 2 ½ cups (592 ml)

- 2-15 oz. (425 g) can cannellini beans, drained and rinsed
- 3 tablespoons (45 ml) lemon juice
- ½ cup (125 ml) sun-dried tomatoes (12 to 16 pieces), if packed in oil use less olive oil
- 1 tablespoon (15 ml) extra virgin olive oil
- 2 tablespoons (30 ml) dried basil
- 4 cloves garlic, roughly chopped, or ½ teaspoon (2.5 ml) garlic powder
- 1 teaspoon (5 ml) sea salt
- ½ teaspoon (2.5 ml) black pepper

Topping:

- ¼ cup (60 ml) walnuts
- ¼ cup (60 ml) parmesan or Manchego cheese, grated

Preheat the oven to 350°F (177°C).

Prepare the topping by placing walnuts in a blender and pulse until you get fine crumbs. Pour into a small bowl and stir in cheese. Set aside.

Prepare the dip by placing all dip ingredients and 2 tablespoons (30 ml) water into the same food processor, and process until smooth. Spoon the mixture into a baking dish and smooth out the top with the back of the spoon. Sprinkle with topping and bake for 25 minutes, or until slightly golden and hot.

Iron-Rich White Bean Dip

This is another easy to make, economical, and tasty dip if traditional hummus made with chickpeas isn't your preference. I'm sensitive to chickpeas; my body just can't digest them. The seasonings are what make this dip special. The bell peppers and lemon juice are high in vitamin C to help with absorbing iron found in the beans. Serve with vegetables or crackers.

Serves 4 to 6

- 1 can (540 ml) cannellini beans (salt-free, if possible)
- 3 tablespoons (45 ml) fresh lemon juice (1 lemon)
- ¼ cup (60 ml) + 1 tablespoon (15 ml) tahini paste (sesame seed butter)
- ¼ cup (60 ml) parsley, finely chopped, loosely packed
- 1 tablespoon (15 ml) fresh dill
- ⅛ teaspoon (0.5 ml) sriracha or hot sauce
- ¼ - ½ teaspoon (1 to 2.5 ml) salt, depending on desired taste
- 1 large clove fresh garlic, minced

Rinse cannellini beans in a strainer to remove canned juice. Place beans in a food processor and pulse a few times. Add in lemon juice, tahini, parsley, dill, sriracha, salt and pepper to taste and blend until smooth.

Red Lentil and Pepper Dip

Roasting the peppers for this dip gives it a sweeter and smokier flavour. If you're pressed for time, you can purchase roasted peppers from your local deli or buy them in a jar, but making your own is super easy and more flavourful. Removing the skins removes any bitterness that may exist in the pepper. The same is true of the lentils: you can buy the canned variety or make your own as suggested in the recipe. It really comes down to how much time you have.

Makes about 3 cups (750 ml)

- 1 cup (250 ml) dry red lentils
- 2 cups (500 ml) water
- ½ cup (125 ml) roasted red peppers, chopped
- 1 tablespoon (15 ml) white miso
- 1 tablespoon (15 ml) lemon juice
- 1 garlic clove, finely minced
- 3 tablespoons (45 ml) tahini
- ½ teaspoon (2.5 ml) sweet smoked paprika, plus extra for garnish
- 1 tablespoon (15 ml) finely chopped flat-leaf parsley
- Black and white sesame seeds, for garnish

Place lentils in fine-mesh sieve and rinse well under cold water. Place in a medium saucepan with water and bring to a boil over medium-high heat. Reduce heat to medium-low and allow lentils to simmer, uncovered and stirring frequently, until liquid is absorbed and lentils are very tender, about 15 minutes.

In the bowl of a food processor, place cooked lentils, red peppers, miso, lemon juice, garlic, tahini, and paprika. Blend, scraping down the sides of the food processor as needed, until dip is smooth and creamy. Dip may be served immediately or stored in an airtight container in the refrigerator for up to a week.

When ready to serve, transfer to serving dish and garnish with parsley, sesame seeds, and an extra pinch of smoked paprika.

Vintage Bean Salad

This salad was a staple at every large family get together when I was growing up. It's made with canned beans so it's easy to make. The traditional dressing is high in sugar, which probably is why it appealed to the masses, but I've changed the recipe to use raw honey, a sugar substitute like Truvia (made with stevia), or a monk fruit sweetener. You can make this salad a day ahead. In fact, it tastes better the next day.

Serves 6 to 8

- 2 20 oz. (566 g) green beans, drained
- 2 20 oz. (566 g) cans yellow beans, drained
- 1 15 oz. (425 g) can kidney beans, drained and washed
- 2 medium onions, diced
- 1 sweet pepper, diced (green looks good)

Dressing:

- 1 cup (250 ml) vinegar
- ½ cup (125 ml) raw honey, monk fruit, or other sugar substitute such as Truvia
- ½ cup (125 ml) avocado oil
- 1 teaspoon (5 ml) salt
- ½ teaspoon (2.5 ml) pepper

Mix the beans and vegetables together in a bowl. Make dressing by mixing the ingredients together and then pour over the bean mixture until evenly coated.

Lentil Sloppy Joes

Sloppy Joes were a special treat when we were kids, usually when Mom was running out of grocery money. Using lentils instead of ground beef makes it even more economical. This version also sneaks more vegetables into your diet. Substitute the traditional white bun for a multi-grain sourdough, gluten free bun, or a lettuce wrap and it becomes an even healthier meal.

Serves 14

- 2 tablespoons (30 ml) olive oil
- 1 large sweet onion, chopped
- 1 medium green pepper, chopped
- 1 medium red pepper, chopped
- 1 medium carrot, diced
- 6 cloves garlic, minced
- 1 ½ cups (375 ml) vegetable or chicken broth
- 1 cup (250 ml) dried red lentils or equivalent canned lentils
- 2 tablespoons (30 ml) chili powder
- 2 tablespoons (30 ml) yellow mustard
- 4 ½ teaspoon (22.5 ml) apple cider vinegar
- 2 teaspoons (10 ml) honey or sugar substitute
- 1 ½ teaspoon (7.5 ml) tomato paste
- ¼ teaspoon (1 ml) salt
- ⅛ teaspoon (0.5 ml) pepper
- **Buns to serve for sandwiches, or lettuce leaves**

In a large skillet, heat oil over medium-high heat. Add onion, peppers, and carrots and cook until crisp but tender. Add garlic, cook for 1 minute longer.

Add broth and lentils, bringing to a boil. Reduce heat, simmer uncovered until lentils are tender, about 15 minutes, or if using canned lentils cook until lentils are heated through. Stir in chopped tomatoes, tomato paste, chili powder, mustard, vinegar, honey, and salt and pepper. Bring to a boil. Reduce heat, simmer until thickened, about 5 to 10 minutes.

Serve on buns or in a lettuce wrap.

Butternut Squash and White Bean Soup

Butternut squash soup is one of my favourites. In this version the beans add fiber and protein. If you don't like chickpeas, leave them out. The quinoa on top is a fun, tasty addition that adds some texture.

Serves 4

- 1 large butternut squash
- 2 tablespoons (30 ml) olive oil
- 1 onion, chopped
- 2 cloves garlic, finely chopped
- 1 tablespoon (15 ml) ginger, finely chopped
- 6 cups (1500 ml) chicken or vegetable broth
- 6 sprigs fresh thyme
- 1 15 oz. (425 g) can white beans, rinsed
- 1 15 oz. (425 g) can chickpeas, rinsed (optional)
- ½ cup (125 ml) quinoa
- ¼ cup (60 ml) pistachios, roughly chopped
- ¼ cup (60 ml) cilantro, roughly chopped
- 1 scallion, sliced

Cut the neck off the squash, peel and cut into ½ inch (1.27 cm) pieces. Heat 1 tablespoon (15 ml) olive oil in a non-stick skillet on medium. Add squash and cook, covered, stirring occasionally, 8 minutes.

Meanwhile, in a Dutch oven on medium heat, cook chopped onion in 1 tablespoon (15 ml) oil, covered, stirring occasionally, 6 minutes. Stir in garlic and ginger, cook for 1 minute. Add chicken broth, fresh thyme, and squash and bring to a boil.

Using a fork, mash white beans and add to soup along with chickpeas.

Cook ½ cup (125 ml) quinoa per package directions; fluff with fork and fold pistachios and cilantro, dried apricots and scallion.

Serve soup topped with quinoa mixture.

Superfood Soup with Veggies and Lentils

This is a hearty vegetable soup with a tomato base. Green lentils have a nutty flavour and keep their shape when cooked, making them excellent to use in soups and salads. They're high in B vitamins so they're good for the brain and your mood.

Makes 10 cups (2½ litres)

- 1 tablespoon (15 ml) avocado oil
- 1 medium onion, finely chopped
- 3 stalks celery, finely chopped
- 2 medium carrots, finely chopped
- 1 medium red, yellow, or orange pepper, finely chopped
- 2 cloves garlic, minced
- 1 ¼ teaspoon (6 ml) sea salt, or more to taste
- ¼ teaspoon (1 ml) ground black pepper, or more to taste
- 1 8 oz. (227 g) container of white or Bella mushrooms, roughly chopped
- 1 tablespoon (15 ml) tomato paste
- 1 cup (250 ml) canned crushed tomatoes
- 6 cups (1500 ml) vegetable or chicken broth
- 1 ½ cups (375 ml) canned green lentils, rinsed and drained
- 4 to 5 sprigs of thyme
- 1 bay leaf
- 1 to 2 cups (500 ml) baby spinach leaves, chopped
- 1 to 2 tablespoons (30 ml) finely chopped parsley

Place oil in a big stock pot over medium heat and sauté onions and celery. Add garlic and sauté for another minute or so, then add carrots, peppers, and mushrooms. Season with salt and pepper. Add in tomato paste, tomatoes, and broth. Add lentils, thyme, and bay leaf. Bring soup to a boil and then turn the heat down to low and let soup simmer until vegetables are soft.

Add the spinach and parsley and serve.

Mushroom Lentil Bolognese

This is a good recipe to hide mushrooms and peppers if you have a fussy eater on your hands, and it only takes about 20 minutes to throw together. Feel free to add in other veggies like carrots, zucchini, or asparagus.

Serves 6 to 8

- 2 tablespoons (30 ml) extra virgin olive oil
- 2 cups (500 ml) sweet onion, diced
- 3 large garlic cloves, minced
- ¼ to ¾ teaspoon (1 to 4 ml) sea salt, plus a pinch
- 16 oz. (450 g) cremini mushrooms, sliced
- 1 teaspoon (5 ml) dried oregano
- 1 teaspoon (5 ml) dried basil
- 1 teaspoon (5 ml) dried thyme
- 14 oz. (400 g) fusilli gluten free pasta
- 3 cups (750 ml) chunky marinara sauce
- 1 (14 oz./398 ml) can lentils, drained and rinsed, or 1 ½ cup (375 ml) cooked lentils
- ¾ cup (175 ml) jarred roasted red peppers, drained and chopped
- 2 tablespoons (30 ml) "runny" tahini
- ½ teaspoon (2 ml) freshly ground black pepper
- ½ teaspoon (2 ml) red pepper flakes (optional)

Bring a large pot of water to a boil for the pasta.

In a large saucepan, heat the oil over medium heat. Add the onion, garlic, and a pinch of salt and stir. Sauté for 4 to 5 minutes until the onion is softened. Stir in the mushrooms, oregano, basil, and thyme and cook for 7 to 8 minutes over medium-high heat, until most of the water cooks off.

When the water for pasta boils, add the pasta and cook according to package instructions.

Into the mushroom mixture, stir in the marinara sauce, lentils, and roasted red pepper until combined. Stir in the tahini. Simmer over medium heat, uncovered, for a few more minutes.

Drain the pasta and rinse with cold water. Stir the pasta into the lentil-veggie mixture until thoroughly combined. Taste and season with salt, pepper, and red pepper flakes. Heat for a couple of minutes, or until cooked through.

Serve and enjoy.

Susanne's Tip: Dice the mushrooms and reduce the amount for kids who don't like them. They'll be undetectable!

Turkey-Lentil Meatloaf with Orange-Roasted Veggies

Serving the roasted veggies with this meatloaf makes this a meal worthy of guests or a special occasion. The meatloaf is moist and the vegetables so delectable you'll definitely want seconds. You don't have to stick to broccoli and sweet potatoes; cauliflower, asparagus, or Brussels sprouts are just a few more options.

Serves 8

- 1 cup (250 ml) gluten free quick-cooking organic rolled oats
- ½ cup (125 ml) milk (any type, unsweetened if plant-based)
- 2 tablespoons (30 ml) tomato paste
- 1 tablespoon (15 ml) apple cider vinegar
- 1 teaspoon (5 ml) gluten free Worcestershire sauce
- 2 pounds (900 g) lean ground turkey
- 1 cup (250 ml) cooked brown lentils, drained and rinsed if using canned
- 2 large organic eggs
- ½ of an onion, finely diced
- 1 carrot, grated
- 2 garlic cloves, minced
- ½ teaspoon (2 ml) dried thyme
- ¼ teaspoon (1 ml) ground nutmeg
- ¼ teaspoon (1 ml) salt

Orange-Roasted Veggies:

- ⅓ cup (80 ml) orange juice
- 2 tablespoons (30 ml) extra-virgin olive oil
- 1 teaspoon (5 ml) tamari or gluten free soy sauce
- 3 medium sweet potatoes, unpeeled, cut into ¼ inch (0.6 cm) rounds
- 2 heads broccoli, cut into florets

Arrange oven racks to accommodate 2 trays. Preheat the oven to 350°F (180°C).

In a medium bowl, mix oats and milk. Set aside for 10 minutes. In a small bowl, mix tomato paste, vinegar, and Worcestershire sauce. Set aside.

In a large bowl, mix turkey, lentils, eggs, onion, carrot, garlic, thyme, nutmeg, and salt. Stir in soaked oats and milk. Mix everything until combined. Form into a loaf about 2 ½ inch (6 cm) high, in a 9 x 13-inch (23 x 33 cm) glass or ceramic casserole dish. Coat top with tomato paste mixture.

Bake on a lower oven rack for 1 hour, or until the thermometer inserted in the centre reads 160° F (70°C). Remove from the oven and allow to cool for 5 minutes before slicing. While meatloaf is cooking, prepare sweet potatoes and broccoli.

In a large bowl, combine all orange-roasted veggie ingredients. Pour onto a large baking sheet and roast on the upper oven rack for 40 to 45 minutes, until vegetables are tender (add to the oven after the meatloaf has been in the oven for 20 minutes).

Slice meatloaf and serve along side roasted vegetables.

Tips for Making a Great Meatloaf:

1. Try using a variety of meat and bean combinations. Try ground beef and kidney beans or turkey and black beans or ground pork and baked beans.
2. Over mixing leads to a tough loaf. Handle with care.
3. Explore different spices. Salt and pepper are great but garlic salt and red pepper make your loaf sing.
4. Consider adding a filling of vegetables, cooked mushrooms or goat cheese.
5. Let your meatloaf rest before serving.

Beautiful Berries and Fabulous Fruits

Berries are one of those superfoods that live up to the hype, especially when we talk about brain health. Recent studies indicate that berry consumption is up, probably due to both the media attention surrounding them and the research that supports their benefits. Berries are a nutritional powerhouse full of vitamins, minerals, and fiber and they're a source of flavonoids and carotenoids. These micronutrients account for their antioxidant and anti-inflammatory effects. Not only do these nutrients help repair damaged cells, the anthocyanins found in red, blue, and purple berries cross the blood-brain barrier to protect our cells from aging.

Berries have been shown to improve memory, slow the aging process, and slow the progression of dementia. Make berries a part of your healthy diet and have a serving each day to boost your brain function.

Fruits are good for you, especially when eaten in their whole, natural form. Oranges, bell peppers, kiwi, guava, and berries contain a high amount of vitamin C, which prevents brain cell damage and supports overall brain health. I believe it's important to keep your vegetable-fruit ratio under control. In other words, eat at least three times the amounts of vegetables to your fruit intake and all will be well.

Lastly, I know a lot of people love to drink their fruit in a smoothie, but masticating the fruit reduces its nutritional value and starts your day with a sugar high.

Did you know that Gala and Red Delicious apples are highest in antioxidants?

Strawberry Rhubarb Compote

Rhubarb is rich in antioxidants and anthocyanins just like berries, so with this pairing you get double the benefits. It also contains proanthocyanidins, which make it anti-bacterial, anti-inflammatory, and anti-cancer and excellent for the brain. I love tart and sweet together so this combination is one of my favourites. Rhubarb is available from the spring to early summer and is super easy to grow in your garden.

Serves 6

- 2 cups (500 ml) fresh rhubarb (cut into ½ inch pieces), or use frozen
- 2 cups (500 ml) fresh strawberries, thickly sliced, or use frozen
- ⅓ cup (75 ml) local raw honey
- 1 tablespoon (15 ml) orange juice or water
- 1 teaspoon (5 ml) grated orange rind
- ½ teaspoon (2.5 ml) cinnamon (optional)
- ½ teaspoon (2.5 ml) vanilla (optional)

In a medium saucepan, combine rhubarb, honey, and orange juice; bring to a boil over medium heat, stirring occasionally. Reduce heat and simmer, until rhubarb is tender. Stir in strawberries, orange rind, cinnamon and vanilla. Turn off heat, cover, and let stand for 5 minutes.

Serve over yogurt.

Berry Chia Seed Jam

Every once in a while, I miss jam on toast. I've purchased sugar-free jams and found the best ones were those made with chia seeds. When I discovered that these jams are easy to make at home, I tried a variety of recipes and liked this one the best.

Makes 1 ⅓ to 1 ½ cups (325 to 375 ml)

- 2 cups (500 ml) fresh or frozen fruit (berries, cherries, peaches, plums, pineapple, kiwi)
- 2 tablespoons (30 ml) chia seeds
- 1 tablespoon (15 ml) freshly-squeezed lemon juice
- 1-2 tablespoons (15 - 30 ml) raw honey, maple syrup, or other sweetener (if needed)

Optional add-ins:

- ½ teaspoon (2.5 ml) vanilla extract
- Lemon zest
- Pinch of cinnamon, ginger, or nutmeg

Heat the berries in a small saucepan over medium-high heat, stirring occasionally, until the fruit is heated through and begins to break down and bubble. Using a masher, mash the fruit until desired consistency.

Stir in the chia seeds and lemon juice until combined. Add sweetener to taste if needed.

Give the jam one final stir. Then serve immediately or transfer to a sealed container and refrigerate for up to 1 week or freeze for up to 3 months.

Susanne's Tip: Fruit infused water is a great way to start the day.
Try lemon water first thing in the morning.

Blueberry Banana Muffins

These muffins have healthy nuts loaded with omega 3 and vitamin E. Essential minerals are found in the honey and chia seeds, and there's a nice number of soluble fibers and healthy fats. You can change up the berries – raspberries, blackberries, or even strawberries work. Just remember to use fresh fruit instead of frozen. *Did you know that if you roll your berries and fruit in flour before adding them to your mixture that they won't sink to the bottom of your baked goods?*

Makes 12

- 1 ½ cups (375 ml) organic rolled oats
- 5 ½ tablespoons (82.5 ml) coconut oil
- 1 cup (250 ml) organic almonds
- ½ cup (125 ml) organic walnuts, chopped
- 2 tablespoons (30 ml) chia seeds
- 2 teaspoons (10 ml) baking powder
- ¼ teaspoon (1 ml) baking soda
- 2 organic eggs, plus 1 egg white
- 1 cup (250 ml) goat or coconut milk yogurt
- 2 teaspoons (10 ml) ground cinnamon
- Zest of ½ a lemon
- ¼ cup (60 ml) local, raw honey
- 2 medium ripe bananas
- 1 cup (250 ml) organic fresh blueberries

Preheat the oven to 350°F (177°C).

Lightly grease a 12-cup muffin pan with 1 ½ tablespoons (22.5 ml) coconut oil. Using a food processor or blender, grind the oats and almonds to a flourlike texture. In a large bowl, combine the ground oats and almonds, walnuts, chia seeds, baking powder and baking soda.

In a separate bowl, lightly beat the eggs. Add the yogurt and stir until combined.

In a small saucepan, add the rest of the coconut oil, cinnamon, lemon zest, and honey and cook over low heat until it has a syrupy consistency.

Add the egg mixture to the dry ingredients and stir. Add the coconut-oil mixture.

Mash the bananas and add to batter and then fold in blueberries. Place equal amounts in the prepared muffin tin. Bake for 20 to 25 minutes or until the toothpick comes out clean.

Orange and Grapefruit Salad

You can use different types of oranges such as blood oranges, tangerines, Seville, mandarin, cara cara, or clementines for this salad. I feel the fruit is sweet enough without maple syrup but it does offer a unique flavour profile.

8 servings

- 2 grapefruit
- 4 navel oranges
- Juice of 1 lemon
- ½ teaspoon (2.5 ml) each ground cinnamon and nutmeg
- 2 tablespoons (30 ml) maple syrup (optional)

With a sharp knife, peel the oranges and grapefruit. Remove peel and as much of the pith as possible. Next, holding the fruit in your hand, cut next to the tough membranes so the flesh is removed in one segment.

Drop the segments into glass serving bowls. Squeeze lemon juice over the citrus segments. Add the spices and maple syrup, if using. Toss gently. Let sit for an hour to blend flavours.

Broiled Grapefruit

This is another vintage recipe converted to make it healthier. People used to load their grapefruit with sugar and then broil it to caramelize the sugar. Using honey or maple syrup is a healthier option and the added spices give it pizazz and a higher nutrient content. This is not a recipe I would make daily but it's great for an occasional treat or impressive dessert.

2 servings

- ½ grapefruit per person
- 1 tablespoon (15 ml) maple syrup per half
- ½ teaspoon (2.5 ml) vanilla per half
- Pinch of cardamom, nutmeg, and cinnamon for each half

Preheat the oven to broil. Place the rack 4 inches (10 cm) below the element.

Cut grapefruit in half and place in a pan or casserole dish. Drizzle fruit with vanilla and maple syrup. Season with spices. Broil for approximately 5 minutes, watching carefully.

Apple Nachos

If you're looking for a treat but are striving to stay away from baked goods, these nachos may hit the spot. Easy to make, they satisfy your sweet tooth and have a nice crunch.

Serves 4

- 2 large apples, cut in half and cored
- 3 tablespoons (45 ml) sunflower or any other nut or seed butter
- 1 tablespoon (15 ml) coconut oil
- 2 tablespoons (30 ml) honey, maple syrup, or stevia blend
- ¼ cup (60 ml) almonds, coarsely chopped
- ¼ cup (60 ml) pecans, coarsely chopped
- ¼ cup (60 ml) dark chocolate bits
- ¼ cup (60 ml) unsweetened coconut flakes

Slice both apples thinly and place one layer of apples on a plate.

Put the butter, oil and sweetener in a saucepan and heat over low heat until melted and mixed. Using a spoon, drizzle this mixture over the apples. Top with almonds, pecans, and dark chocolate. Repeat until all ingredients are used.

Diced Avocado Guacamole

My sister brought this guacamole to a family event and we devoured it within minutes. I love avocados and finding new ways to enjoy them. This recipe has become my go to for potlucks and entertaining. You really taste the actual avocados.

Serves 4

- 2 to 4 ripe avocados, diced

Dressing

- ¼ cup (60 ml) extra virgin oil
- 2 tablespoons (30 ml) fresh lemon juice
- 2 tablespoons (30 ml) red wine vinegar
- 2 - 3 cloves garlic, minced
- ¼ cup (60 ml) cilantro, finely chopped
- ¼ cup (60 ml) flat leaf parsley, finely chopped
- ½ teaspoon (2.5 ml) crushed red pepper flakes
- ½ teaspoon (2.5 ml) dried oregano
- 1 teaspoon (5 ml) sea salt
- ¼ teaspoon (1 ml) freshly cracked black pepper

Mix all dressing ingredients well. Toss with diced avocados.

Devilishly Good Dark Chocolate Desserts

Eating healthy doesn't mean that you have to totally give up treats or sweets; you just need to be selective and choose wisely. After all, we all want an occasional treat or want to celebrate a birthday or event with a cake. Dark chocolate is the answer. There are many benefits of chocolate for brain health. It's been shown to improve blood flow to the brain and improves cognitive function in elderly people with dementia.

Dark chocolate is full of nutrients including 11 grams of fiber, 67% of the RDI of iron, as well as magnesium, copper, manganese, potassium, phosphorus, zinc, and selenium. It's also a powerful source of antioxidants. Other health benefits include lowering blood pressure, improving cholesterol levels, and lowering heart disease risk. Interesting fact: the flavonoids in chocolate may protect your skin from damaging sun rays.

Although dark chocolate is good for you, most chocolate bars have some amount of sugar and preservatives in them unless you buy the 100% chocolate type. Shop wisely, read the label and make your own desserts and chocolates. Search for recipes with cocoa rather than chunks so you can control the type and amount of sugar. Remember that chocolate is an occasional treat to be enjoyed in small quantities.

Chocolate Avocado Fudge

This decadent slice of fudge is easy to make and uses creamy avocado. If you can't find healthy chocolate chips (Lilly brand) break a dark chocolate bar into pieces.

- 2 cups (500 ml) creamy nut butter
- ½ cup (125 ml) chocolate chips
- ½ cup (125 ml) mashed avocado (about ½ an avocado)
- ½ cup (125 ml) sweet potato (cooked)
- ¼ cup (60 ml) coconut milk
- 2 tablespoons (30 ml) maple syrup
- 3 tablespoons (45 ml) cacao powder

Preheat the oven to 350°F (190°C).

Grease a loaf pan. Combine all ingredients except chocolate chips. Pour into the pan. Add the chocolate chips to the batter and bake for 20 minutes. Keep leftovers refrigerated.

Simple Chocolate Ramekin Cakes

When I'm stressed, I'm a "see food – eat food" type of person, so making foods in smaller quantities helps me control my portions. These little cakes are just enough for our family. Easy and delicious, they're made nutritious with almond meal and maple syrup (which has more antioxidants than any fruit or vegetable you can buy).

Yield: 3 small cakes

- 3 oz. (86 g) dark chocolate
- ¼ cup (60 ml) plus 1 tablespoon (15 ml) coconut oil
- ½ cup (125 ml) maple syrup
- 2 large eggs
- 1 cup (250 ml) almond meal

Preheat the oven to 350°F (176°C).

Combine the chocolate, coconut oil, and maple syrup in a small saucepan over low heat, stirring continuously until the chocolate is completely melted, about 3 to 5 minutes. Remove the pan from the heat.

Whisk the eggs together in a medium bowl and add to the chocolate mixture. Add the almond meal and continue to mix until all ingredients are incorporated.

Lightly grease three 7-ounce (198 g) ramekins with coconut oil. Pour the batter evenly into each ramekin. Bake for 20 minutes and serve immediately.

Almond Butter Balls

I have yet to find a cookie that's gluten and sugar free that rivals the real thing, but balls can be a good substitute and are a great energy food for camping, hiking, or those long days when lunch is delayed. Substitute the almond butter for peanut or cashew butter and you have a whole different taste. These are a good way to use up your butters if they've been hanging around too long in your cupboard.

Makes 12–15 balls

- 1 cup (256 g) almond butter
- 2 tablespoons (30 ml) honey
- 1 teaspoon (5 ml) vanilla extract
- 1 teaspoon (5 ml) sea salt
- ½ cup (125 ml) + 1 tablespoon (15 ml) coconut flour
- ¾ cup (180 g) dark chocolate chips
- 1 tablespoon (15 ml) coconut oil

Combine the almond butter, vanilla, salt, and coconut flour and mix until a dough forms.

Roll the dough into small balls about 1 inch (2.5 cm) in diameter and place on a paper lined baking sheet. Refrigerate for 30 to 60 minutes or until very firm.

Once the balls are ready, melt the chocolate chips and coconut oil in a small saucepan over low heat. Stir continuously until completely melted, about 4 to 6 minutes. Remove from heat.

Use a toothpick to stab the balls and dip them into the melted chocolate. Place them on the baking sheet.

Refrigerate for a minimum of 20 to 30 minutes. Store in the refrigerator.

Susanne's Tip: Cook with Love. It's more important than what you cook.
Energy transfers into our food.

Chocolate Espresso Clusters

If you're a coffee and chocolate fan...these are divine. Toast your nuts over low heat for a short amount of time or go with raw nuts. Both work! Packaged nicely, they make a great gift for friends and family. They have quite a bit of caffeine in them, so refrain from eating the whole batch in one sitting.

Makes 2 cups (500 ml)

- 3 oz. (90 g) bittersweet chocolate, finely chopped
- 2 teaspoons (10 ml) espresso powder
- ½ cup (125 ml) toasted whole almonds
- ½ cup (125 ml) cashews
- ¾ teaspoon (3.7 ml) flaked sea salt

Melt the chocolate with the espresso powder in a pan over moderate heat until smooth. Stir in the almonds and cashews until coated. Transfer with a spatula onto a parchment-lined baking sheet, spreading them out. Sprinkle with ½ to ¾ teaspoon (5 to 7 ml) salt and chill until set.

Break into pieces before serving.

Tasty Teas

Anyone who knows me knows that I am a "tea-aholic" (not sure if this is actually a word, but I like it!). I love all kinds of teas. There are so many different types and they all have their own functions and unique properties that make them beneficial for our brain, our mood, and our overall health. There are teas that lift our spirits, teas that calm us down, teas that improve our memory, and teas that keep our immune system strong. There are teas that help us detox and teas that are antioxidant, anti-inflammatory, and anti-bacterial.

For example, the antioxidants in green tea prevent oxidative stress that destroy free radicals, and ginkgo biloba tea boosts mental clarity and retention. Peppermint tea affects Gaba receptors in the brain, which helps decrease our stress response and helps us sleep better. Ginseng helps us when we are tired and lacking energy. There are teas that are adaptogens*, like ashwagandha, and tulsi that help with mood.

Tea is also a good alternative to juices and processed drinks and tastes delicious both hot and cold. Fermented teas like kombucha have the same effect as other probiotics with the added benefits from the tea it's made from.

Whichever tea you choose, your brain and body will benefit. Just remember that many teas contain caffeine, so if you are sensitive to caffeine, drink them before noon or stick to herbal teas like rooibos or chamomile. Buy organic and be aware of packaging if you are buying teas in a tea bag versus loose tea. Many popular tea brands use plastic to seal their tea bags and this plastic releases many nanoplastic particles into the water. You are literally drinking plastic. Choose tea that's in biodegradable, plastic free, organic or plant based bags. Don't be fooled by "silk" tea bags. They are almost always made of plastic and take years to biodegrade. Paper tea bags should be compostable and oxygen bleached without the use of chemicals. Avoid tea bags held together with glues, staples, or non organic string.

*Adaptogens are herbal pharmaceuticals. Ashwagandha, rhodiola rosea, and licorice are all examples of adaptogens. They work to counteract the effect of stress on the body.

Lemon Ginger Elderberry Tea

This recipe starts with a base of tea and is really an excuse to get the healing benefits of the cinnamon, fennel, and ginger. Elderberries are a superfood craze that will continue to gain in popularity due to their high immunity boosting properties. They reduce inflammation and help you deal with stress. Any herbal tea can be used for the base.

Serves 1

- 1 ½ cups (350 ml) filtered water
- 1 cinnamon stick
- 1 star anise, or ¾ teaspoon (4 ml) fennel seed
- 3 slices peeled ginger root
- 1 herbal tea bag, such as lemon ginger
- 1 tablespoon (15 ml) organic elderberry syrup or 2 tablespoons (30 ml) dried elderberries
- Raw honey, to taste (optional)

In a small saucepan, combine all ingredients except for the tea bag and elderberry syrup. Bring to a boil, reduce heat to low and simmer, covered for 15 minutes.

Remove from heat. Add herbal tea bags. Steep for 5 minutes. Strain into a cup. Add honey if using.

Digestive and Cleansing Tea

This isn't real tea in the traditional sense, but for years our ancestors have cooked herbs and plants to make a broth to help us benefit from the herbs and spices. This is a cleansing tea that can be used to detox and aid in digestion.

Serves 1

- 1 tablespoon (15 ml) cumin seeds
- 1 tablespoon (15 ml) coriander seeds
- 1 tablespoon (15 ml) fennel seeds
- 4 cups of water

Boil for 5 minutes.

Garlic Tea Tonic

Garlic is a magical herb that is widely used around the world as a tonic for the whole body. It has been used for everything from reducing cholesterol to fighting infections. Garlic is full of antioxidants that protect and reverse cell damage.

Serves 1

- 4 large garlic cloves, roughly chopped
- 1 cup (250 ml) boiling water
- ½ lemon, juiced
- 1 tablespoon (15 ml) apple cider vinegar
- Honey to taste

Put the garlic cloves in the cup of boiling water, cover, and steep for a few minutes. Add the lemon juice, vinegar, and honey. Sip slowly.

Garlic Ginger Lemon Drink

This drink is similar to the previous one but with the addition of ginger, another powerful medicinal superfood. It's an antioxidant and anti-inflammatory and controls blood sugar levels.

Serves 1

- **1 to 3 medium/large garlic cloves**
- **Ginger root (same size as garlic cloves)**
- **½ lemon (large) or 1 small**
- **Pinch of cayenne pepper powder**

Into a cup, grate the garlic cloves and ginger root and squeeze in the lemon juice. Add in the cayenne pepper. Add the warm water. Drink immediately after fixing first thing in the morning on an empty stomach.

Blueberry Green Iced Tea

Here the blueberries are paired with green tea for a refreshing iced tea that you'll enjoy serving in the summer. No one needs to know that they're preventing neurodegenerative diseases when they drink it! Green tea has been studied in the prevention of both Alzheimer's and Parkinson's and there seems to be some merit to the claims that it keeps the brain functioning properly.

Serves 1

- 1 green tea bag
- ½ cup (125 ml) fresh or frozen blueberries
- 2 teaspoons (30 ml) lemon juice
- 1 lemon slice

Put the tea bag in 1 cup (250 ml) of boiling water. Let steep for 5 minutes. Remove the tea bag and pour the tea, blueberries, and lemon juice into a blender and blend for less than a minute. Strain and pour into a glass with ice. Garnish with a slice of lemon.

Susanne's Tip: You can freeze actual slices or fruit or berries to put in glasses of iced tea or water to keep the drink cold while adding flavour. Similarly, you can pour freshly squeezed fruit juice into an ice cube tray and freeze until ready to use.

Iced Licorice Tea

There are approximately 300 bioactive compounds in the licorice root. It's believed to have neuroprotective properties due to its anti-inflammatory and antioxidant levels. It has a laxative effect so a great option if you are experiencing constipation from poor food choices or stress. Too much may cause cardiovascular side effects, so stick to a serving a day.

1 serving

- 3 large mint springs
- 3 3-inch-long (7.62 cm) strips of orange peel
- ¾ cup (175 ml) boiling water
- 2 licorice spice tea bags
- Glass of ice

Garnish: thin orange wedge, sprig of mint. Glass of ice

Crush 3 mint sprigs between your fingers and place them in a cup, add orange peel, and pour the boiling water over them. Add 2 licorice spice tea bags and steep 8 minutes. Remove tea bags and pour tea into an ice-filled glass. Garnish with orange slice and mint

Chai Tea Chia Seed Pudding with Warm Apple Topping

I love chai tea but can't tolerate black tea. Any caffeine makes me hyper and affects my sleep. Thankfully, there are blends available with rooibos or green teas. Whichever you use, this pudding with warm apples will hit the spot after spending time outside or when you are in need of comfort food.

Serves 4

Pudding:
- 1 ½ cups (375 ml) unsweetened almond milk
- ½ teaspoon (2 ml) vanilla
- 4 chai tea bags or chai rooibos tea bags
- ½ cup (125 ml) chia seeds
- ½ teaspoon (2 ml) cinnamon
- 2 teaspoons (10 ml) pure maple syrup or to taste

Warm Apples:
- 2 crisp red apples
- 1 tablespoon (15 ml) fresh lemon juice
- 2 teaspoons (10 ml) virgin coconut oil
- 2 teaspoons (10 ml) pure maple syrup
- ¼ teaspoon (1 ml) cinnamon
- ¼ cup (60 ml) pecans, toasted and crushed

Make the pudding in a small saucepan over medium heat. Place almond milk in pan and heat over medium heat. Add the tea bags, turn off the heat, cover the pot, and steep the tea until it cools to room temperature. Remove the tea bags after squeezing them to release all flavour. Discard the bags.

Transfer the mixture to a 24-ounce (750 ml) container with a lid. Stir in chia seeds, vanilla and cinnamon. Refrigerate 3 hours or overnight. In the morning, stir in maple syrup.

Warm the apples by cutting them into slices. In a medium bowl, toss the pieces in lemon juice. Melt the coconut oil in a large skillet over medium-high heat. Add the maple syrup and apples and gently toss, cooking until slightly softened and golden brown. Remove from heat and sprinkle with cinnamon. To assemble, divide pudding among 4 glasses and top with apples and crushed pecans.

Susanne's Tip: Break the soda habit by drinking lemon water, apple cider vinegar water, homemade vegetable juices, or herbal tea.

Conclusion

I hope that I've convinced you that what you eat influences how you feel as well as who you are. We are what we eat! Nutrition is important to keep all parts of our body healthy, including our brain, and although it's not the only line of defense against neurodegenerative disease and mental health…it is an important one.

In this book I've offered alternatives to processed, chemical-laden foods that are convenient but detrimental to our health and well-being. The better you eat, the healthier you will be and the happier you will be. I see it with my clients on a daily basis. Healthy people enjoy life!

Eat for Health. Eat for Joy!

Susanne

11 Other Ways to Care for Your Mental Health

1. See a therapist
2. Improve your sleep habits
3. Drink lots of pure water
4. Exercise
5. Do the right kind of yoga
6. Nurture friendships
7. Avoid toxic relationships
8. Shut down negative self-talk
9. Learn stress management techniques
10. Take regular vacations
11. Spend time at the ocean or in the water

"We delight in the beauty of the butterfly, but rarely admit the changes it has gone through to achieve that beauty."

Maya Angelou

References

1. Iati, M. (2019, October 31). *He was acting drunk but swore he was sober. turns out his stomach was brewing its own beer.* The Washington Post. Retrieved February 6, 2022, from https://www.washingtonpost. Com/health/2019/10/24/he-was-acting-drunk-swore-he-was-sober-turns-out-his-stomach-was-brewing-its-own-beer/

2. Oz, M. (2017, May). Feeling Tired and Hangry? *Dr. Oz Magazine*, 42–42.

3. The nurse in England that created the program CITA is Pam Armstrong. She wrote a small book called Back to Life: The Great Escape from Tranquilliser Addiction. Available free in PDF format at http://www. Citap. Org. Uk/BackToLife. Pdf

4. Bryson, B. (2020). The body: *A guide for occupants* (pp. 239–239). Essay, Anchor Canada.

5. Centers for Disease Control and Prevention. (2022, January 24). *Chronic diseases in America*. Centers for Disease Control and Prevention. Retrieved February 6, 2022, from https://www. Cdc. Gov/chronicdisease/resources/infographic/chronic-diseases. Htm

6. World Health Organization. (2004). (Publication). *The Global Burden of Disease* (p. 44). Switzerland.

7. Fox, M. (2016, December 12). *One in 6 Americans take antidepressants, other psychiatric drugs: Study.* NBCNews. Com. Retrieved February 6, 2022, from https://www. Nbcnews. Com/news/amp/ncna695141

8. Wise, R. A. (1974). Lateral hypothalamic electrical stimulation: Does it make animals 'hungry'? *Brain Research*, 67(2), 187–209. http://www. Sciencedirect. Com/science/article/pii/0006899374902728

9. Keys, A. (1950). The biology of human starvation. *University of Minnesota*. https://doi. Org/https://www. Opa. Org/monitor/2013/10/hunger

10. *Weight issues*. Weight Loss and Nutrition Program | Dr. Daniel Amen. (n. D.). Retrieved February 6, 2022, from https://www. Amenclinics. Com/conditions/weight-loss-and-nutrition/

11. *Poll finds most N. Y. doctors think nutrition education should be required for physicians*. Physicians Committee for Responsible Medicine. (n. D.). Retrieved February 6, 2022, from https://www. Pcrm. Org/news/news-releases/poll-finds-most-ny-doctors-think-nutrition-education-should-be-required

12. ScienceDaily. (2019, April 3). *Globally, one in five deaths are associated with poor diet*. ScienceDaily. Retrieved February 6, 2022, from https://www. Sciencedaily. Com/releases/2019/04/190403193702. Htm

13. Selhub, E. (2020, March 26). *Nutritional strategies to ease anxiety*. Harvard Health. Retrieved February 6, 2022, from https://www. Health. Harvard. Edu/blog/nutritional-psychiatry -your-brain-on-food-201511168626

14. El Ansari, W., Adetunji, H., & Oskrochi, R. (2014). Food and Mental Health: Relationship between Food and Perceived Stress and Depressive Symptoms among University Students in the United Kingdom. *Central European Journal of Public Health*, 22(4). 10.21101/cejph. A3941

15. Slykerman, R. F., Hood, F., Wickens, K., Thompson, J. M. D., Barthow, C., Murphy, R., Kang, J., Rowden, J., Stone, P., Crane, J., Stanley, T., Abels, P., Purdie, G., Maude, R., & Mitchell, E. A. (2017, October). *Effect of lactobacillus rhamnosus HN001 in pregnancy on postpartum symptoms of depression and anxiety: A randomised double-blind placebo-controlled trial*. EBioMedicine. Retrieved February 6, 2022, from https://ww. Ncbi. Nlm. Nih. Gov/pmc/articles/PMC5652021/#__ffn-sectitle

16. Jones, A. M. (2020, October 30). *Quebec professor's drink to treat mild cognitive impairments in older adults hitting store shelves*. CTVNews. Retrieved February 16, 2022, from https://www. Ctvnews. Ca/health/quebec-professor-s-drink-to-treat-mild-cognitive-impairments-in-older-adults-hitting-store-shelves-1.5167186

17. Newport, M. T. (2015). *The coconut oil and low-carb solution for Alzheimer's, Parkinson's, and other diseases*. Basic Health Publications, Inc.

18. Bauman, M. A. (2005). *Fight fatigue: Six simple steps to maximize your energy*. Tate Publishing.

19. Bryson, B. (2019). *The Body: A Guide for Occupants*. Penguin Random House.

20. Tartagni, M., Cicinelli, M., Tartagni, M., Alrasheed, H., Matteo, M., Baldini, D., Del Salvia, M., Loverro, G., & Montagnani, M. (2016). Vitamin D Supplementation for Premenstrual Syndrome-Related Mood Disorders in Adolescents with Severe Hypovitaminosis D. *Journal of Pediatric and Adolescent Gynecology*, 29(4), 357–361. https://doi. Org/10.1016/j. Jpag.2015.12.006

21. Holick, M. F. (2007). Vitamin D Deficiency. *The New England Journal of Medicine*, 266–281.

22	Khoraminya, N., Tehrani-Doost, M., Jazayeri, S., Hosseini, A., & Djazayery, A. (2012, October 23). *Therapeutic effects of vitamin D as adjunctive therapy to fluoxetine in patients with major depressive disorder.* The Australian and New Zealand journal of psychiatry. Retrieved February 6, 2022, from https://pubmed. Ncbi. Nlm. Nih. Gov/23093054/
23	Amini, S., Jafarirad, S., & Amani, R. (2018). Postpartum depression and vitamin D: A systematic review. *National Library of Medicine.* https://doi. Org/10. 1080/10408398.2017.1423276
24	Moscani, L. (2019). *In Brain Food: The Surprising Power of Eating for Cognitive Power* (p. 266). essay, Avery Publishing.
25	Grundy, S. R. (2017). *In The Plant Paradox: The Hidden Dangers in "Health" Foods that Cause Disease and Weight Gain.* essay, HarperCollins.
26	Crowther, S. (2015). *The No Recipe Cookbook: A Beginners Guide to the Art of Cooking.* Skyhorse Publishing.
27	John Hopkins Center for a Livable Future. (2014, November 17). *Study suggests home cooking is a main ingredient in healthier diet.* Center for a Livable Future. Retrieved February 6, 2022, from https://clf. Jhsph. Edu/about-us/news/news-2014/study-suggests-home-cooking-main-ingredient-healthier-diet

Index

A

ADHD 11, 15, 18
Alcohol 4, 19
Allspice 48, 81
Almond Butter 188
Almond Milk 202
Almonds 11, 41, 43, 44, 45, 48, 60, 81, 172, 178, 190
Alzheimer's 9, 12, 23, 200, 211
Amaranth 20, 24
Anchovy 72
Antioxidants 23, 24, 38, 82, 84, 112, 166, 168, 182, 187, 192, 198
Anxiety 1, 2, 5, 6, 7, 9, 10, 11, 13, 14, 15, 16, 17, 18, 19, 211
Apples 20, 24, 58, 90, 166, 178, 202
Arrowroot 20, 91, 92, 136
Artichokes 72
Artificial Sweeteners 10, 11, 19, 21
Arugula 22, 54, 64, 69, 75, 76, 106
Asparagus 17, 20, 22, 41, 113, 116, 118, 160, 162
Autism 11
Avocado 22, 38, 40, 66, 72, 76, 77, 82, 90, 91, 108, 126, 128, 136, 140, 142, 144, 149, 154, 158, 180, 184

B

Bananas 15, 17, 24, 46, 172
Barley 20, 21
Basil 23, 66, 118, 120, 151, 160
Beans 15, 21, 22, 23, 52, 69, 100, 146, 147, 149, 150, 151, 152, 154, 156, 169
Beef 15, 18, 77, 97, 136, 139, 155, 169
Beef stock 77, 97, 155, 169
Beets 17, 24, 84, 102, 104, 108, 110
Berries 17, 23, 166, 168, 171, 172, 200
Black Beans 146, 150
Blood sugar 1, 6, 14, 23, 43, 52, 72, 146, 147, 199
Blueberries 46, 123, 172, 200
Brain-Gut connection 12
Brazil 43
Breads 2, 21, 115, 132, 149
Broccoli 17, 20, 22, 58, 65, 75, 100, 136, 139, 162, 164
Brussel sprouts 22, 75, 79, 142, 162
B Vitamins 16, 24, 158

C

Cabbage 20, 22, 58, 64, 75, 77, 78, 82
Caffeine 7, 10, 11, 19, 24, 190, 192, 202
Cannellini Beans 69, 146, 147, 151, 152
Cardamom 45, 48, 58, 176
Carrots 2, 24, 58, 82, 84, 86, 90, 96, 97, 98, 101, 103, 104, 106, 108, 155, 158, 160
Cauliflower 20, 22, 75, 77, 81, 102, 162
Celery 20, 22, 65, 102, 104, 110, 158
Chai 48, 202
Cheese 2, 5, 11, 15, 33, 34, 36, 41, 53, 54, 69, 70, 103, 106, 108, 115, 120, 122, 125, 126, 128, 131, 151, 169
Chia Seeds 48, 171, 172, 202
Chicken 5, 18, 54, 79, 97, 101, 116, 142, 144, 155, 156, 158
Chicken broth/stock 54, 155, 156, 158
Chickpeas 52, 60, 69, 86, 146, 152, 156
Chocolate 4, 18, 24, 44, 178, 182, 184, 187, 188, 190
Cinnamon 44, 45, 46, 48, 50, 58, 62, 97, 98, 103, 142, 144, 168, 171, 172, 174, 176, 194, 202
Cloves 34, 41, 48, 52, 54, 72, 86, 90, 97, 104, 115, 116, 136, 140, 151, 155, 156, 158, 160, 162, 180, 198, 199
Cocoa 48, 182
Coconut 9, 11, 17, 36, 44, 46, 48, 56, 58, 60, 66, 82, 90, 91, 92, 103, 120, 123, 126, 136, 149, 172, 178, 184, 187, 188, 202, 211
Corn 2, 16, 19, 20, 21, 23, 53, 135, 136
Cranberry 142, 144
Cruciferous vegetables 22, 75, 82
Cucumber vii, 22, 65, 131, 132, 134
Cumin 52, 101, 150, 197
C Vitamins 17, 23, 90, 152, 166

D

Dates 45
Dementia 9, 12, 17, 166, 182
Depression 1, 2, 6, 7, 9, 10, 11, 14, 15, 16, 17, 18, 19, 23, 64, 211, 212
Desserts 182
Digestion 19, 52, 56, 75, 122, 146, 197
Dill 104, 110, 125, 131, 132, 152
DNA 12
Dopamine 14, 15, 50
D Vitamins 14, 15, 16, 22, 211, 212

E

Eggs 16, 17, 18, 21, 23, 31, 33, 34, 36, 38, 40, 41, 46, 53, 70, 77, 103, 120, 140, 162, 164, 172, 187
Elderberry 194
Energy Levels 10
Espresso 190

F

Fat 14, 18, 19, 23, 31, 40, 41, 43, 64, 123, 143
Fatty Acids 16, 24, 43, 127, 135
Fermented Foods 11, 15, 17, 118, 122
Feta Cheese 125, 128, 131
Fiber 13, 22, 23, 24, 38, 43, 52, 64, 72, 75, 84, 122, 146, 147, 150, 156, 166, 182
Fish 15, 16, 17, 18, 23, 25, 82, 127, 128, 131
Fish Oil 16
Flavonoids 22, 23, 24, 110, 166, 182
Flours 20, 21
Fructose 103
Fruits 9, 17, 20, 23, 24, 70, 112, 166

G

GABA 15
Garlic 22, 32, 33, 34, 38, 41, 52, 54, 69, 70, 72, 81, 82, 86, 90, 91, 92, 94, 97, 98, 104, 115, 116, 120, 125, 131, 136, 140, 150, 151, 152, 153, 155, 156, 158, 160, 162, 164, 169, 180, 198, 199
Ghee 23, 40, 76, 97, 98, 136
Ginger 22, 23, 48, 66, 82, 84, 90, 102, 136, 156, 171, 194, 199
Glucose 1, 6, 14, 23, 43, 52, 72, 146, 147, 199
Gluten-free 53, 126, 149
Gnocchi 91, 92
Goat cheese 41, 106, 115, 169
Grains 9, 16, 19, 20, 21, 24, 69, 120, 147
Granola 44
Grapefruit 174, 176
Grapes 20, 65
Green Onions 125, 131
Greens (leafy green vegetables) 33, 64
Green teas 202
Gribiche 132, 134
Guacamole 180

H

Harissa Paste 86
Hazelnuts 106, 108
Herbs 23, 98, 132, 134, 197
Honey, organic 48, 66, 79, 118, 123, 154, 155, 168, 171, 178, 194
Hormones 1, 7, 10, 11, 15, 17, 20, 50, 135
Horseradish 22, 32, 75, 104
Hummus 50, 52, 86, 152

I

Immune System 12, 13, 43, 122, 192
Inflammation 1, 9, 12, 13, 15, 16, 17, 19, 20, 21, 24, 25, 43, 146, 194
Iodine 10, 17
Iron 11, 18, 23, 24, 126, 146, 152, 182

J

Jam 171

K

Kale 11, 20, 25, 33, 58, 64, 65, 75

L

Lectins 21, 22, 146
Legumes 15, 21, 23, 146, 147
Lemon 32, 52, 54, 58, 72, 81, 86, 100, 104, 106, 108, 116, 118, 125, 128, 131, 151, 152, 153, 171, 172, 174, 180, 194, 198, 199, 200, 202, 208
Lentils 19, 23, 147, 153, 155, 158, 160, 162, 164
Lettuce 70, 125, 155
Lettuces 22
Licorice 21, 192, 201
L-theanine 18

M

Macadamia 43, 48
Magnesium 10, 12, 14, 16, 22, 23, 24, 146, 182
Manchego 151
Maple syrup 46, 48, 58, 66, 104, 118, 171, 174, 176, 178, 184, 187, 202
Mayonnaise 32, 72, 110, 128
Meat 10, 16, 19, 20, 24, 77, 79, 82, 98, 135, 139, 140, 169
Metabolism 10, 17, 19
Milk 17, 36, 38, 41, 44, 45, 48, 58, 91, 92, 96, 97, 98, 116, 123, 126, 162, 164, 172, 184, 202
Minerals 11, 12, 22, 23, 24, 58, 126, 140, 166, 172
Miso 17, 21, 122, 153
Mood disorders 1, 11, 15, 211
Muffins 172
Mushrooms 14, 15, 20, 22, 36, 38, 77, 120, 158, 160, 165, 169

N

Nachos 178
Nervous System 12, 13, 14, 15, 16, 17
Non-starchy vegetables 22
Norepinephrine 14, 17

Nut Butter 62, 184
Nuts 5, 16, 23, 43, 44, 48, 58, 61, 62, 66, 70, 103, 104, 123, 126, 172, 190

O

Oatmeals 15, 56, 123, 124
Oats 20, 22, 24, 44, 56, 58, 123, 162, 164, 172
Obesity 7, 8
Oils 11, 16, 19, 23, 53, 61, 62, 66, 104, 136
Olive oil 16, 32, 33, 34, 41, 50, 52, 53, 54, 64, 69, 70, 72, 79, 81, 84, 86, 91, 92, 96, 100, 101, 102, 104, 106, 108, 110, 115, 120, 125, 128, 131, 132, 134, 151, 155, 156, 160, 162
Omegas 16
Omelettes 34, 36
Onions 17, 20, 22, 36, 69, 76, 84, 87, 94, 97, 98, 104, 125, 131, 150, 154, 158
Oranges 17, 24, 142, 166, 174
Oregano 66, 81, 94, 120, 125, 140, 142, 160, 180
Oxytocin 14, 15

P

Panko Bread Crumbs 132
Parsley 22, 84, 90, 94, 97, 101, 104, 108, 128, 132, 134, 142, 156, 158, 160, 162, 164, 194, 197
Pasta 5, 19, 54, 96, 160
Peanuts 17, 21, 23, 61
Peas 20, 23, 97, 98, 113, 116, 147
Pecans 44, 62, 70, 103, 178, 202
Pepper 17, 22, 32, 33, 34, 36, 38, 40, 41, 52, 54, 58, 61, 68, 69, 70, 72, 76, 77, 79, 81, 82, 86, 90, 92, 94, 96, 97, 98, 100, 101, 102, 106, 108, 110, 113, 115, 116, 118, 120, 125, 128, 131, 132, 134, 136, 139, 140, 142, 144, 149, 151, 152, 153, 154, 155, 158, 160, 169, 180, 199
Peppers 14, 20, 25, 152, 153, 155, 158, 160, 166
Pesticides 7, 10, 19, 20
Pizza 5, 53, 92, 120
Polyphenols 23
Potatoes 2, 17, 21, 24, 25, 76, 84, 91, 94, 96, 97, 98, 162, 164

Potatoes, Sweet 76, 94
Prebiotics 13, 17
Preservatives 3, 7, 10, 19, 23, 32, 53, 97, 182
Probiotics 9, 13, 15, 17, 122, 192
Processed Foods 1, 3, 6, 19
Proteins 6, 9, 17, 18, 19, 20, 21, 23, 24, 31, 36, 38, 43, 48, 52, 61, 70, 100, 126, 140, 146, 147, 150, 156
Pumpkins Seeds 50, 52, 58, 100, 101, 123

Q

Quiche 38, 41
Quinoa 19, 20, 24, 100, 136, 156

R

Radish 22, 75, 132, 134
Raspberries 23, 123, 142, 172
Refined flours 3, 5, 19, 21, 38, 41, 46, 61, 91, 92, 103, 120, 126, 172, 188
Rhubarb 168
Rice 19, 21, 22, 24, 77, 136, 139, 146
Root Vegetables 24, 84, 104

S

Sage 23, 41, 91, 92, 142
Salads 27, 50, 58, 69, 100, 146, 158
Salmon 11, 15, 16, 25, 79, 82, 128, 132, 134
Seafood 17, 18, 25, 127, 131
Seeds 16, 18, 23, 43, 48, 50, 52, 58, 66, 70, 81, 100, 101, 120, 123, 136, 153, 171, 172, 197, 202
Serotonin 11, 14, 15, 16, 17, 18, 50, 122, 140
Sesame 18, 82, 136, 139, 152, 153
Shallots 22, 108, 116
Shepherds pie 97
Shitake mushrooms 14, 15, 20, 22, 36, 38, 77, 120, 158, 160, 165, 169
Soups 21, 23, 27, 50, 84, 90, 116, 146, 147, 158
Soy 17, 18, 19, 21, 22, 23, 53, 68, 126, 136, 162
Spaghetti 120

Spices 32, 34, 48, 60, 66, 68, 81, 101, 115, 128, 140, 144, 147, 169, 174, 176, 197
Spinach 14, 20, 25, 33, 34, 64, 70, 72, 90, 158
Squash 17, 22, 41, 90, 100, 120, 156
Sriracha 152
Standard American Diet 7, 18
Steak 76, 135, 136
Stevia 46, 48, 154, 178
Stir fry 123
Strawberries 20, 23, 168, 172
Sugar 1, 2, 3, 6, 7, 10, 11, 12, 14, 18, 19, 22, 23, 24, 43, 46, 52, 66, 72, 103, 134, 135, 146, 147, 154, 155, 166, 171, 176, 182, 188, 199
Sun-Dried 151
Supplements 5, 15, 18, 72
Sweet Pea 20, 116
Swiss chard 25, 64, 65

T

Tahini paste 152
Tamari 68, 162
Tapioca Flour 21
Tapioca Starch 20, 146
Teas 23, 192, 202
Tisanes 23
Tofu 16, 18, 81, 126
Tomatoes 14, 20, 21, 22, 25, 34, 69, 70, 76, 77, 96, 113, 115, 149, 150, 151, 155, 158
Toxins 4, 20, 22, 75, 97
Tryptophan 18, 140
Turkey 18, 79, 97, 116, 140, 162, 164, 169
Turmeric 23, 48, 50, 66, 84, 90, 101

V

Vegan 91, 126
Vegetable broth 54, 77, 90, 102
Vegetable oil 16, 19, 53, 61, 136
Vegetables 2, 3, 9, 17, 20, 22, 23, 24, 36, 50, 52, 58, 64, 65, 70, 75, 82, 84, 86, 96, 101, 102, 104, 112, 113, 116,

120, 122, 125, 150, 152, 154, 155, 158, 162, 164, 166, 169
Vegetarianism 77
Vinegar 11, 23, 24, 32, 58, 65, 66, 68, 69, 70, 76, 82, 106, 108, 110, 113, 115, 131, 132, 134, 136, 154, 155, 162, 164, 180, 198, 208
Vitamins 11, 12, 14, 16, 22, 23, 24, 58, 126, 140, 158, 166

W

Walnuts 16, 43, 48, 54, 58, 70, 103, 104, 151, 172
Wasabi 61, 75
Water 17, 22, 25, 34, 52, 54, 58, 64, 72, 77, 81, 92, 96, 98, 104, 108, 110, 113, 118, 131, 142, 144, 147, 150, 151, 153, 160, 168, 171, 192, 194, 197, 198, 199, 200, 201, 206, 208
Wheat 3, 20, 21

Y

Yogurt 17, 18, 23, 50, 58, 101, 104, 118, 122, 123, 124, 125, 168, 172

Z

Zinc 15, 18, 50, 126, 146, 147, 182
Zucchini 22, 38, 140, 160

www.ingramcontent.com/pod-product-compliance
Lightning Source LLC
Chambersburg PA
CBHW051310110526
44590CB00031B/4360